Estimating the Query Difficulty for Information Retrieval

Estimating the Query Difficulty for Information Retrieval

David Carmel and Elad Yom-Tov

ISBN: 978-3-031-01144-3   paperback
ISBN: 978-3-031-02272-2   ebook

DOI 10.1007/978-3-031-02272-2

A Publication in the Springer series
SYNTHESIS LECTURES ON INFORMATION CONCEPTS, RETRIEVAL, AND SERVICES

Lecture #15
Series Editor: Gary Marchionini, *University of North Carolina, Chapel Hill*
Series ISSN
Synthesis Lectures on Information Concepts, Retrieval, and Services
Print 1947-945X   Electronic 1947-9468

Synthesis Lectures on Information Concepts, Retrieval, and Services

Editor

Gary Marchionini, *University of North Carolina, Chapel Hill*

Synthesis Lectures on Information Concepts, Retrieval, and Services is edited by Gary Marchionini of the University of North Carolina. The series will publish 50- to 100-page publications on topics pertaining to information science and applications of technology to information discovery, production, distribution, and management. The scope will largely follow the purview of premier information and computer science conferences, such as ASIST, ACM SIGIR, ACM/IEEE JCDL, and ACM CIKM. Potential topics include, but are not limited to: data models, indexing theory and algorithms, classification, information architecture, information economics, privacy and identity, scholarly communication, bibliometrics and webometrics, personal information management , human information behavior, digital libraries, archives and preservation, cultural informatics, information retrieval evaluation, data fusion, relevance feedback, recommendation systems, question answering, natural language processing for retrieval, text summarization, multimedia retrieval, multilingual retrieval, and exploratory search.

Estimating the Query Difficulty for Information Retrieval
David Carmel and Elad Yom-Tov
2010

iRODS Primer: Integrated Rule-Oriented Data System
Arcot Rajasekar, Reagan Moore, Chien-Yi Hou, Christopher A. Lee, Richard Marciano, Antoine de Torcy, Michael Wan, Wayne Schroeder, Sheau-Yen Chen, Lucas Gilbert, Paul Tooby, and Bing Zhu
2010

Collaborative Web Search: Who, What, Where, When, and Why
Meredith Ringel Morris and Jaime Teevan
2009

Multimedia Information Retrieval
Stefan Rüger
2009

Estimating the Query Difficulty for Information Retrieval

David Carmel and Elad Yom-Tov

IBM Research, Israel

SYNTHESIS LECTURES ON INFORMATION CONCEPTS, RETRIEVAL, AND SERVICES #15

ABSTRACT

Many information retrieval (IR) systems suffer from a radical variance in performance when responding to users' queries. Even for systems that succeed very well on average, the quality of results returned for some of the queries is poor. Thus, it is desirable that IR systems will be able to identify "difficult" queries so they can be handled properly. Understanding why some queries are inherently more difficult than others is essential for IR, and a good answer to this important question will help search engines to reduce the variance in performance, hence better servicing their customer needs.

Estimating the query difficulty is an attempt to quantify the quality of search results retrieved for a query from a given collection of documents. This book discusses the reasons that cause search engines to fail for some of the queries, and then reviews recent approaches for estimating query difficulty in the IR field. It then describes a common methodology for evaluating the prediction quality of those estimators, and experiments with some of the predictors applied by various IR methods over several TREC benchmarks. Finally, it discusses potential applications that can utilize query difficulty estimators by handling each query individually and selectively, based upon its estimated difficulty.

KEYWORDS

information retrieval, retrieval robustness, query difficulty estimation, performance prediction

Contents

Acknowledgments

We have relied on many insightful research works for this lecture, and we thank all researchers cited in this paper for their great work on query difficulty. In particular, the Ph.D. theses of Vishwa Vinay (55), Yun Zhou (69), and Claudia Hauff (21), were a major invaluable source for us. We especially thank them for their thorough research which we found to be extremely useful in preparing this book. In addition, Section 5.5 on prediction sensitivity is based on joint work with Anna Shtok and Oren Kurland. We thank them for letting us publish this work, as it has not been published yet elsewhere. We are, however, fully responsible to any remaining errors in interpretation and presentation.

We thank Gary Marchionini and Diane D. Cerra from Morgan & Claypool for inviting us to write this lecture. We would also like to thank our colleagues and managers from IBM Research in Haifa for allowing us to take the time for writing. We especially thank Nadav Har'El, Haggai Roitman, Ian Soboroff, and Oren Kurland, for their great comments and suggestions on a draft of this manuscript.

Finally, but not least, this book was mostly written during evenings and weekends. We thank our families for supporting us and for their great patience. We dedicate this book to them, with love.

David Carmel and Elad Yom-Tov
Haifa, Israel, 2010

CHAPTER 1

Introduction – The Robustness Problem of Information Retrieval

The exponential growth of digital information that is available on the Web, and on other existing digital libraries, calls for advanced search tools that will be able to satisfy users who seek for reliable knowledge for their information needs. Indeed, many information retrieval (IR) systems have emerged over the last decades that are able to locate precise information even from collections of billions of items. Search engine tools have become the leading channels for professionals, as well as the general public, for accessing information and knowledge for their daily tasks.

However, most IR systems suffer from a radical variance in retrieval performance when responding to users' queries, as measured by the quality of returned documents. Even for systems that succeed very well on average, the quality of results returned for some of the queries is poor. This may lead to user dissatisfaction since individual users only care about the effectiveness of the system for their own requests and not about the system's average performance.

The variability in performance is due to a number of factors. There are factors related to the query itself, such as term ambiguity. For example, consider the ambiguous query *Golf*. Without any context search engines will be unable to identify the desired information need (the sport or the car). In such cases, poor results are expected as answers related to different meanings of the query are interleaved. Other factors are related to the discrepancy between the query language and the content language (also known as the *vocabulary mismatch problem*) when inconsistency exists between the way users express their needs and the way the content is described. Other problematical cases are *missing content queries*, for which there is no relevant information in the corpus that can satisfy the information needs.

The experimental results of state-of-the-art IR systems participating in TREC[1] show a wide diversity in performance among queries. Most of the systems, even with high precision on average, fail to answer some of the queries. For example, consider the TREC query (58) *"Hubble Telescope Achievements"*, which was found to be difficult for most TREC participants. For this query, many of the irrelevant documents retrieved by typical search engines deal with budget constraints, scheduling

---

[1] The Text REtrieval Conference (TREC) is sponsored by the National Institute of Standards and Technology (NIST) and the U.S. Department of Defense. Its purpose is to support research within the IR community by providing the infrastructure necessary for large-scale evaluation of text retrieval methodologies.

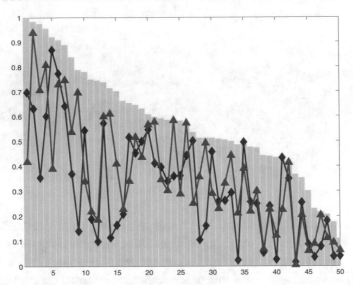

Figure 1.1: The variance in performance among queries and systems. Queries are sorted in decreasing order according to the highest performance (average precision) achieved among all TREC participants (shown in gray bars). The performance of two different systems per query is shown by the two curves. Based on (19).

problems, and other issues related to the Hubble telescope project in general; but the gist of that query, *achievements*, is lost.

On the other hand, diversity in performance also exists among participating systems who answer the same query. For some of the queries, some of the systems succeed very well while other completely fail. This is probably due to system dependent factors such as the specific retrieval methodology and implementation details. Figure 1.1 shows the high variance in performance (the average precision, defined in Chapter 2), of two different systems for several TREC queries. Queries are sorted in decreasing order according to the highest performance among all TREC participants (shown in gray bars). The performance of two different systems per query is shown by the two curves. The figure clearly shows the high variability in systems' performance over the queries, as well as the high diversity in performance per query among the systems.

The high diversity in performance among queries, as well as among systems, led to a new research direction termed *query performance prediction (QPP)* or *query difficulty estimation (QDE)*. The challenge is to predict in advance the quality of the search results for a given query, retrieved by a given retrieval system, when no relevance information is given by a human operator. Such a performance prediction will let IR systems to better serve "difficult" queries and to decrease variability in performance. If we could determine in advance which retrieval approach would work well for a given query, then hopefully, selecting the appropriate retrieval method on a query basis could improve the retrieval effectiveness significantly.

1.1 REASONS FOR RETRIEVAL FAILURES - THE RIA WORKSHOP

The *Reliable Information Access* (RIA) workshop (20) was the first attempt to rigorously investigate the reasons for performance variability between queries and systems. The goal of the RIA workshop was to understand the contributions of both system variability factors and query variability factors to overall retrieval variability. The workshop brought together seven different IR systems and assigned them to common IR tasks. By performing extensive failure analysis of the retrieval results for 45 TREC topics[2], nine failure categories were identified. Table 1.1 presents the failure categories, each associated with an example topic, as they appear in the workshop summary. Five categories of the nine relate to the systems' failure to identify and cover all aspects of the topic. Other categories are mostly related to failures in query analysis.

One of the RIA workshop's conclusions was that the root cause of poor performance is likely to be the same for all systems. It is well known fact that, in general, different retrieval methods are retrieving different results for the same query, but according to the failure analysis, all systems fail for the same reasons, for most topics.

Another conclusion was that the systems' inability to identify all important aspects of the query would seem to be crucial and one of the main obstacle in successfully handling the information needs. The failure to emphasize one aspect of a query over another, or the opposite, to emphasize one aspect and neglect other aspects, accounted for several of the reasons for failure. This type of failure is demonstrated by the TREC topic *"What disasters have occurred in tunnels used for transportation?"*. Exposing the relation between *disasters* and *tunnels*, the main aspect to be answered in this query, is not trivial as text analysis is required for that. Moreover, emphasizing only one of these terms (for example, due to its relative rarity) will deteriorate performance because each term on its own does not fully reflect the information need. Similarly, the *spotted owl episode* which is mentioned in the example of failure category 5, should be identified as redundant for successful retrieval since the theme to be answered for this topic is wildlife conservation in other countries (excluding the U.S.).

A surprising result was the finding that the majority of failures could be fixed with traditional IR techniques such as better relevance feedback mechanism and better query analysis that gives guidance as to the relative importance of the query terms and their inner relationship. Furthermore, if a failure is identified, and the reason is explained to the person submitting the query, he may be able to revise the query so as to alleviate the problem. For example, the query *"Hubble telescope achievements"* might be changed to enforce the word *"achievements"* to appear in the retrieved documents. A simple query modification such as this can dramatically improve retrieval performance.

---

[2]A "topic" in TREC defines a specific information need. The query submitted to the search engine is inferred from the given topic. Different query formulation rules can be used to construct queries from the topic.

Table 1.1: RIA Topic Failure Analysis Categorization. From (9).

Category	Topic example
1. General technical failure (stemming, tokenization)	*Identify systematic explorations and scientific investigations of Antarctica, current or planned.* (Systems fail to stem "Antarctica" and "Antarctic" to the same stem (root).)
2. All systems emphasize one aspect; missing another required term	*What incidents have there been of stolen or forged art?* (All systems missing "art".)
3. All systems emphasize one aspect; missing another aspect	*Identify documents discussing the development and application of spaceborne ocean remote sensing.* ("Ocean" should be emphasized and expanded.)
4. Some systems emphasize one aspect; some another; need both	*What disasters have occurred in tunnels used for transportation?* ("Disasters" and "tunnels" should both be emphasized.)
5. All systems emphasize one irrelevant aspect; missing point of topic	*The spotted owl episode in America highlighted U.S. efforts to prevent the extinction of wildlife species... What other countries have begun efforts to prevent such declines?* (Systems wrongly emphasize "spotted owl' and "US efforts".)
6. Need outside expansion of "general" term (e.g., expand Europe to individual countries)	*Identify documents that discuss the European Conventional Arms Cut as it relates to the dismantling of Europe's arsenal.*
7. Need query analysis to determine relationship between query terms	*How much sugar does Cuba export and which countries import it?* (Need quantity analysis and relationships between ' "Cuba", "sugar", and "export".)
8. Systems missed difficult aspect that would need human help	*What are new methods of producing steel?* (Need interpretation of "new methods".)
9. Need proximity relationship	*What countries are experiencing an increase in tourism?* (Aspects of "increase" and "tourism" should be close together.)

The goal of performance prediction is first and foremost to identify failure, using some of the hints identified above, as well as others. A next logical step is to try and identify the cause of failure and correct it. Nowadays, most query prediction methods focus on identifying failure. It is still an open challenge to identify the exact failure modes for a given query. If systems could estimate what failure categories the query may belong to, it is likely that systems could apply specific automated techniques that correspond to the failure mode in order to improve the system performance.

1.2   INSTABILITY IN RETRIEVAL - THE TREC'S ROBUST TRACKS

The diversity in performance among topics and systems led to the TREC Robust tracks in the years 2003-2005 (57; 58; 59), which encouraged systems to decrease variance in query performance by focusing on poorly performing topics. Systems were challenged by 50 old TREC topics found to be "difficult" for most systems over the years. A topic is considered difficult in this context when the median of the average precision scores of all participants for that topic is below a given threshold (i.e., half of the systems are scored lower than the threshold), but there exists at least one high outlier score.

Systems were evaluated by new measures (discussed in Chapter 2) that emphasize the systems' least effective topics, thus encouraging participants to identify difficult topics and to handle them appropriately. The most useful of these metrics was geometric MAP (GMAP), which uses the geometric mean instead of the arithmetic mean when averaging precision values. The geometric mean emphasizes the lowest performing topics (44), and it is thus a useful measure for the system's robustness as measured over the set of topics, i.e., the system's ability to confront difficult queries.

Several approaches to improving the effectiveness of poor topics were tested, including a selective query processing strategy based on performance prediction, post-retrieval reordering, selective weighting functions and selective query expansion. While each of these techniques can help some of the queries, none of them was able to show consistent improvement over traditional non-selective approaches. The leading retrieval methods utilized the web as an external resource to expand (all) queries (58). Apparently, expanding the query by appropriate terms extracted from an external collection can increase the effectiveness of many queries, including poorly performing queries.

In the Robust tracks of 2004 and 2005 systems were asked, as a second challenge, to additionally predict their performance (i.e., the average precision) for each of the testing topics. The TREC topics were then ranked according to their predicted value, and evaluation was done by measuring the similarity between the predicted performance-based ranking and the actual performance-based ranking. Prediction methods suggested by the participants varied from analyzing the scores of the top results, analyzing the frequency distribution of query terms in the collection, and learning a predictor using old TREC queries as training data. The (poor) prediction results clearly demonstrated that measuring performance prediction is intrinsically difficult; the measured similarity between predicted topic ranking and actual topic ranking was low for most runs submitted to the track. Moreover, fourteen runs had a negative correlation between the predicted and actual topic rankings.

On the positive side, the difficulty in developing a reliable performance prediction methods, publicized that challenge to the IR community and attracted the attention of many researchers.

In order to get an idea how difficult the performance prediction task is, we can attempt to assess how difficult this task is for human experts. An experiment in this spirit was conducted in TREC-6 (60), estimating whether human experts can predict the query difficulty. A group of experts were asked to classify a set of TREC queries to three degrees of difficulty – easy, middle, hard, based on the query expression only. These judgments were compared to the "usual" difficulty measure of a query, the median of the average precision scores, as determined after evaluating the performance of all participating systems. The Pearson correlation between the expert judgments and the "true" values was very low (0.26). Moreover, the agreement between experts, as measured by the correlation between their judgments, was very low too (0.39). The low correlation with the true performance patterns, and the lack of agreement among experts, illustrate how difficult this task is and how little is known about what makes a query difficult.

One of the questions to answer in the Robust track of 2005 was whether queries found to be difficult in one collection are still considered difficult in another collection. Difficult queries in the ROBUST collection were tested against another collection (the AQUAINT collection (59)). The median average precision of all participants over the 50 queries for the ROBUST collection is 0.126 compared to 0.185 for the same queries over the AQUAINT collection. Assuming that the median score of all participants is a good indication for query difficulty, these results indicate that the AQUAINT collection is *"easier"* than the ROBUST collection, at least for the 50 difficult queries of the Robust track. This might be due to the collection size, due to the fact that there are many more relevant documents for those queries in AQUAINT, or due to the document features such as length, structure, and coherence. Carmel et al. (12) examined whether the relative difficulty of the queries is preserved over the two document sets, by measuring the Pearson correlation between the median precision scores of the 50 difficult queries as measured over the two datasets. The Pearson correlation is 0.463, which shows some dependency between the median scores of a topic on both collections. This suggests that even when results for a query are somewhat easier to find on one collection than another, the relative difficulty among topics is preserved, at least to some extent.

1.3   ESTIMATING THE QUERY DIFFICULTY

The high variability in query performance, as well as the TREC robust tracks, have driven a new research direction in the IR field on estimating the quality of the search results, i.e., the query difficulty, when no relevance feedback is given. Estimating the query difficulty is an attempt to quantify the quality of results returned by a given system for the query. An example for such a measure of quality is the average precision (AP) of the query (defined in Chapter 2). Such a query difficulty estimation is beneficial for many reasons:

1. As feedback to the users: The IR system can provide the users an estimation on the expected quality of results retrieved for their queries. The users can then rephrase queries that were found to be "difficult", or alternatively, resubmit a "difficult" query to alternative search resources. Additionally, IR systems can improve their interaction with their users through recommending better terms for query refinement as derived from the analysis of the predicted performance of the refined queries (31).

2. As feedback to the search engine: The search engine can invoke alternative retrieval strategies for different queries according to their estimated difficulty. For example, intensive query analysis procedures that are not feasible for all queries due to time response restrictions, may be invoked selectively for difficult queries only. Moreover, predicted performance can be used for parameter tuning in the absence of training data. Given a sample of training queries with predicted performance, the engine can utilize this data for parameter tuning in order to maximize its performance.

3. As feedback to the system administrator: The administrator can identify queries related to a specific subject that are "difficult" for the search engine and to expand the collection of documents to better answer poorly covered subjects. Identifying *missing content queries* is especially important for commercial search engines which should better identify, as soon as possible, popular emerging user needs that cannot be answered appropriately due to missing relevant content.

4. For IR applications: For example, query difficulty estimation can be used by a distributed search application as a method for merging the results of queries performed distributively over different datasets by weighing the results from each dataset according to their estimated quality. Several potential applications that exploit difficulty estimation are discussed in Chapter 8.

Estimating the query difficulty is a significant challenge due to the numerous factors that impact retrieval performance. As already has been mentioned, there are factors that are related to the query expression (e.g., ambiguity), to the dataset (e.g., heterogeneity), and to the retrieval method. In addition, while traditionally IR research mainly focuses on evaluating the relevance of each document to a query, independently of the other documents, the new performance prediction approaches attempt to evaluate the quality of the whole result list to the query. This complexity burdens the prediction task compared to the retrieval task and calls for new prediction methods that will be able to handle this challenging task.

The notion of query difficulty is usually related to a specific query that is submitted to a specific retrieval method while searching over specific collection. However, query performance can vary over different retrieval methods. Similarly, query performance depends on the collection we search over. Therefore, the "generality" of query difficulty depends on whether this query will be considered difficult by any retrieval method, over any dataset. This generality is usually measured by averaging the predicted query performance of several retrieval methods over several collections. For example, an ambiguous query will probably have high degree of generality as most retrieval methods are expected to perform poorly over most datasets. In contrast, a missing content query is only difficult for specific datasets that do not cover the underlying need. Similarly, we can measure the "difficulty" of a given collection as the average difficulty of a sampled set of queries, while answered by several different retrieval methods.

1.4   SUMMARY

In this chapter, we introduced the robustness problem of IR and reviewed several reasons that cause a query to be considered difficult. We described the taxonomy of failure modes suggested in the RIA workshop and summarized the main results of the TREC Robust tracks. We then discussed several scenarios where query difficulty estimation can be beneficial. The rest of the lecture is organized as follows:

In Chapter 2, we review the basic concepts used in the lecture. In Chapters 3,4,5, we present a new taxonomy for the different types of performance predictors and overview several leading prediction methods suggested in recent years. We summarize several experimental studies on the prediction quality of those query performance predictors over some TREC benchmarks. Chapter 6 discusses how some predictors can be combined together to enhance prediction quality. Chapter 7 provides a general framework for query difficulty. Chapter 8 overviews several IR applications that utilize existing performance predictors for their task. In addition, we discuss the potential of some applications to benefit from performance prediction. Finally, Chapter 9 concludes and discusses open research directions in this emerging field of query performance prediction.

CHAPTER 2

Basic Concepts

Predicting the query performance is the task of estimating the expected quality of the search results, when no relevance information is given. In this chapter, we will define the basic concepts that are used in the rest of the book.

2.1 THE RETRIEVAL TASK

Given a text query q, a collection of documents D, and a retrieval method π, the retrieval task can be formalized as follows:

$$D_q \leftarrow \pi(q, D),$$

π receives q and D as input and retrieves a ranked list of results $D_q \subseteq D$. Many retrieval methods estimate the relevance probability for each document $d \in D$ to q and retrieve the documents with the highest estimation scores, ranked according to these scores. Popular retrieval methods are the vector space *tf-idf* based ranking (47), which approximates relevance by the similarity between the query and a document in the vector space; the probabilistic based *OKAPI-BM25* formula (29), which approximates the document's relevance probability to the query; and a language-model based approach (43), which estimates the probability that the query was generated by the document's language model.

The retrieval quality is usually evaluated by benchmarks such as TREC collections that provide a corpus, a set of topics, and the set of the relevant documents per topic (called Qrels for query relevance set) in the collection. A TREC topic is a statement that describes a specific information need, including a clear description of the criteria that make a document relevant, while a query that is inferred from the topic is the actual text given to the search system. The Qrels is a list of relevant documents to the topic. Given such a benchmark with relevance information, the retrieval quality of a retrieval method π is measured by standard IR quality measures of π's ability to retrieve as many relevant documents from the Qrels (high recall) and to rank them on top of the ranked list (high average precision, defined below).

Popular quality measures are the precision at k (P@k) and the (non-interpolated) average precision (AP) (61). $P@k$ is the fraction of relevant documents in the top-k results. AP is the average of precisions computed at the point of each of the relevant documents in the ranked sequence:

$$AP(q) = \frac{1}{|R_q|} \sum_{r \in R_q} P@rank(r),$$

where R_q is the set of the relevant documents, r is a single relevant document, and $P@rank(r)$ is the precision at the rank position of r. In practical terms, Average Precision is usually calculated from a ranking which is truncated at some rank position (typically 1000 in TREC). In these conditions, for any r which ranks below this truncation point or not at all ($rank(r) > 1000$), $P@rank(r)$ is treated as zero. This is usually a reasonable approximation.

For evaluating systems over many queries, the usual approach is to take the (arithmetic) mean of average precision values over the queries (MAP). An alternative to the (arithmetic) average precision is the geometric mean average precision (GMAP). The geometric mean emphasizes the lowest performing queries (44); therefore, it is more sensitive to the system's robustness in terms of performance variability over a set of topics.

2.2   THE PREDICTION TASK

Given the query q and the result list D_q, the prediction task is then to estimate the retrieval quality of D_q, in satisfying I_q, the information need behind q. In other words, the prediction task is to predict $AP(q)$ when no relevance information (R_q) is given. Throughout this lecture, we will focus on predicting $AP(q)$ at cutoff 1000; other quality measures can be predicted in the same manner.

The performance predictor can be described as a procedure that receives the query q, the result list D_q, and the entire collection D and returns a prediction to the quality of D_q in satisfying I_q, i.e., the expected average precision (AP) for q:

$$\widehat{AP}(q) \leftarrow \mu(q, D_q, D).$$

The quality of a performance predictor μ can be measured over the same benchmarks that are used for retrieval quality estimation. High correlation between the performance prediction values for a given set of queries, with their actual precision values, reflects the ability of μ to successfully predict query performance. The prediction quality is measured by the correlation between the predicted average precision, $\widehat{AP}(q)$, to the actual average precision, $AP(q)$, over a given set of testing queries $Q = \{q_1 \ldots q_n\}$:

$$Quality(\mu) = correl\left([AP(q_1) \ldots AP(q_n)], [\widehat{AP}(q_1) \ldots \widehat{AP}(q_n)]\right).$$

This correlation provides an estimation to prediction accuracy. In the following, we provide an overview of correlation methods, and the interested reader is referred to statistics textbooks for a more thorough discussion of these methods.

2.2.1   LINEAR CORRELATION

There are several methods for measuring the correlation between two variables, which in our case are the actual and predicted values of the target variable. The simplest is the linear, or Pearson, correlation. Given a sample of n actual values of the target variable, $y = (y_1, \ldots, y_n)$, and the corresponding predicted values, $\widehat{y} = (\widehat{y}_1, \ldots, \widehat{y}_n)$, this correlation is defined as:

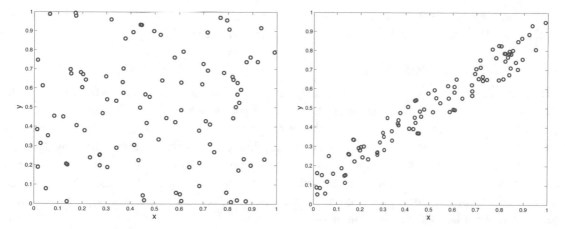

Figure 2.1: Examples of low (left) and high (right) correlation between two variables.

$$r_{y,\widehat{y}} = \frac{\sum_{i=1}^{n} (y_i - avg(y)) (\widehat{y}_i - avg(\widehat{y}))}{(n-1)std(y)std(\widehat{y})}$$

where $avg()$ denotes the sample mean, and $std()$ denotes the sample standard deviation. The correlation $r_{y,\widehat{y}}$ is a number between -1 and $+1$, where -1 denotes perfect anti-correlation, 0 denotes statistical independence, and $+1$ denotes perfect correlation.

Figure 2.1 shows two examples of the correlation between predicted and actual values. The left figure shows the case where there is no relationship between the variables, and correlation is thus low, whereas the right figure shows a high degree of correlation.

It is also common to report the square of r (denoted as R^2) which compares the variance in prediction values with the variance of actual data. Known as the coefficient of determination, it is interpreted as the proportion of variability in the actual values of the target variable that is accounted for by the variability in prediction values. R^2 can be directly computed as follows:

$$R^2 = 1 - \frac{SS_{Err}}{SS_{Tot}} = 1 - \frac{\sum_{i=1}^{n} (y_i - \widehat{y}_i)^2}{\sum_{i=1}^{n}(y_i - avg(y))^2}.$$

Linear correlation is closely related to another metric used for evaluating prediction performance, known as Root Mean Square Error (RMSE). RMSE is computed as follows:

$$RMSE_{y,\widehat{y}} = \sqrt{\frac{1}{n-1} \sum_{i=1}^{n} (y_i - \widehat{y}_i)^2}$$

It can be shown that there is a simple relationship between RMSE and the linear correlation coefficient: RMSE relates to the square root of SS_{Err} in the R^2 equation. It is usually more informative to use the linear correlation coefficient because of the intuitive understanding it provides in terms of the reduction in variance, by normalizing it with the variance of the target variable.

2.2.2 RANK CORRELATION

Linear correlation is easy to measure and is frequently used. However, it also suffers from a significant drawback: Consider the left-hand side of figure 2.1. If one were to add a small number of points at ($y = 100, \widehat{y} = 100$), these would have a relatively large effect on r because of their high values. This would imply that correlation was high, even though this result is affected from only a few points.

Rank, or *Spearman's-ρ* correlation, solves this problem by measuring differences in ranks rather than actual values. Ranks are the indexes of the variables when they are sorted. Usually, instead of computing the Pearson correlation between values, the *Spearman's-ρ* correlation ρ between ranks is calculated using the following equation:

$$\rho_{y,\widehat{y}} = 1 - \frac{6 \sum_{i=1}^{n} d_i^2}{n(n^2 - 1)},$$

where d_i is the difference in ranks between y_i and $\widehat{y}_i$.

A third method for estimating correlation is the *Kendall's-τ* rank correlation. *Kendall's-τ* is a function of the minimum number of swaps between neighboring items needed to produce one rank ordering from the other, i.e., how many neighboring swaps will be needed to convert the rank ordering of the predicted values to that of the actual values. If the minimum number of swaps needed is denoted by Q, the formula for deriving the correlation coefficient is:

$$\tau = 1 - \frac{4Q}{n(n - 1)}$$

It can be shown that *Kendall's-τ* can also be computed from the number of operations required to bring one list to the order of the other list using the *bubble sort* algorithm. The advantage of *Kendall's-τ* is that is easy to gain an intuitive understanding of its meaning, through the number of swapping operations needed.

One of the drawbacks of rank correlation is that while considering the ranking only, the distance between point values is not taken into account. Therefore, it is common practice to report both linear and rank correlations as measures for prediction quality.

2.3 PREDICTION ROBUSTNESS

Measuring the correlation between actual performance (AP) and the predicted performance ($\widehat{AP}$) for a testing query set, as an indication for prediction quality, mostly fits a single system scenario when we wish to estimate the prediction quality of a given performance predictor. This estimation enables the comparison between different prediction methods when applied by the same retrieval system over a fixed set of testing queries and over a fixed dataset. However, the prediction quality is highly dependent on the retrieval method since the target variable (the actual AP) is dependent on the specific retrieval approach. This inherently introduces a difficulty which must be taken into account. For example, it is easy to build a perfect predictor which always succeeds in predicting the failure of a retrieval method that only retrieves random documents. Moreover, the prediction quality also depends on the testing queries and the data collection used for retrieval, as the "difficulty" of the collection may affect retrieval quality (12).

In order to measure the robustness of a predictor, i.e., how well it performs when applied with different retrieval methods, or when applied over different queries and datasets, there are two main approaches. In the first one, the prediction quality is measured and compared over several retrieval methods, over several collections, and over different testing sets of queries. A robust predictor is expected to perform well independently of the retrieval method, the collection, and the query set. Indeed, as we will show in Chapter 4, it is hard to find one predictor that fits all, as most predictors suffer from low prediction robustness.

An alternative approach is to evaluate the predictor's robustness independently of a specific retrieval method. Given many retrieval systems with their search results for a set of testing queries over a given dataset (this is the usual case in TREC ad-hock tracks), in such a framework a query is considered difficult if most systems fail to perform well, i.e., to achieve reasonable AP. The common measure for query difficulty is the median AP of all participating systems. If this median is below a given threshold, we consider this query as difficult. In such a framework, the prediction robustness is measured by the predictor ability to identify those poorly performing queries, i.e., to rank the queries according to their difficulty. Since query difficulty is determined by the performance of all participants, hence it is independent of a specific retrieval method. The prediction quality is then measured by the (linear or rank) correlation between the ranking of queries according to their actual difficulty (the median of participants' AP) and the ranking based on their predicted difficulty. We note that this is much more challenging task since the predictor is not exposed to the retrieval methods used by participants.

2.4   SUMMARY

This chapter covered the main concepts we will use throughout this lecture. We discussed the retrieval task and the standard methodology used in IR for estimating retrieval performance. We then defined the prediction task and how prediction quality can be measured. In the following, we survey various performance prediction methods, of different types, and analyze their prediction ability using those measures for performance prediction quality.

CHAPTER 3

Query Performance Prediction Methods

The high potential of query performance prediction for IR tasks, and the significant challenge involved, has led to many research efforts in developing various prediction methods. Existing prediction approaches are roughly categorized to pre-retrieval methods and post-retrieval methods. Pre-retrieval approaches predict the quality of the search results before the search takes place, thus only the raw query, and statistics of the query terms gathered at indexing time, can be exploited for prediction. In contrast, post-retrieval methods can additionally analyze the search results. Figure 3.1 presents a general taxonomy of existing prediction approaches.

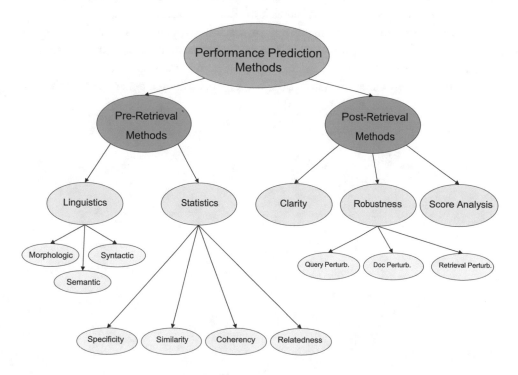

Figure 3.1: A general taxonomy of query performance prediction methods.

Pre-retrieval prediction methods can be classified to linguistic based approaches that apply morphological, syntactical, and semantical analysis in order to identify lexical difficulty of the query. In contrast, statistical methods analyze the statistical features of the query terms such as the occurrence distribution over the documents in collection, query term co-occurrence statistics, and more. The advantage of these methods is that the prediction only relies on early analysis of all terms in the vocabulary, conducted during indexing time. During search, the query performance is predicted using the statistical features of the query terms determined in advance, an inexpensive process that can be applied before the search is carried out.

On the other hand, post-retrieval methods analyze the search results, looking for coherency and robustness of the retrieved documents. We can classify these methods into 1) clarity based methods that measure the coherency (clarity) of the result set and its separability from the whole collections of documents, 2) robustness based methods that estimate the robustness of the result set under different types of perturbations, and 3) score analysis based methods that analyze the score distribution of results.

Post-retrieval methods are usually more expensive as the search results should be analyzed after retrieval, a heavy process that demands some content analysis of the documents. However, these methods are directly applied to the result set thus they are more suitable for identifying inconsistency, incoherency, and other characteristics that reflect low quality. On-the contrary, pre-retrieval methods predict the quality of search results with the lack of direct analysis of the documents' content thus they may be unaware to some flaws in results. In the following, we describe and compare those approaches in more details. Chapter 4, and Chapter 5 afterward, describe and compare several pre and post retrieval methods. Chapter 6 discusses how several prediction methods can be combined together. Chapter 7 summarizes this part of the book by describing a general model for estimating query difficulty.

CHAPTER 4

Pre-Retrieval Prediction Methods

Pre-retrieval prediction approaches estimate the quality of the search results, before the search takes place. Thus, only the query terms, associated with some pre-defined statistics gathered for all the terms in the vocabulary, can be used for prediction. Such methods are easy to compute but are usually inferior to post-retrieval approaches since they do not take the retrieval method into account. The (usually short) query alone is often not expressive enough for reliable prediction of the quality of the search results.

However, the data required by pre-retrieval methods can be calculated during indexing time and does not require the dynamic computation at search time, as post-retrieval methods do. As such, pre-retrieval methods, despite their inferiority, provide effective instantiation of query performance prediction for search applications that must efficiently respond to search requests.

For example, consider the naive pre-retrieval predictor which is based on the query length. The query length is measured by the number of unique non stop-word terms in the query, assuming that longer queries are easier to answer. However, He and Ounis (25) showed that in contrast to the common belief, no correlation exists between query length and query performance. In contrast, handling long queries is difficult as they usually contain a lot of noise. This noise is in the form of extraneous terms that the user believes are important, but in fact are confusing to the retrieval system (4; 32).

Other pre-retrieval methods can be split to linguistic and statistical methods. Linguistic methods apply *natural language processing* (NLP) techniques and external linguistic resources to identify ambiguity and polysemy in the query. Statistical methods analyze the distribution of the query terms within the collection, looking for deviations in the distribution of the query terms frequency. In the following, we elaborate on several pre-retrieval prediction methods from these two categories.

4.1 LINGUISTIC APPROACHES

Linguistic methods analyze the query expression, searching for ambiguity and polysemy as indicators for query difficulty. Mothe and Tangui (40) extracted 16 different linguistic features of the query, looking for significant correlations between these features and the system performance. The query text is analyzed by several linguistic tools such as a morphological analyzer, a shallow parser, and the Wordnet lexical database (18).

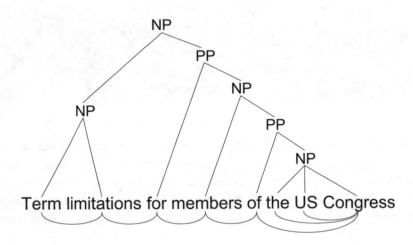

Figure 4.1: Syntactic parse tree of the TREC topic 158: *"Term limitations for members of the US congress"*. NP denotes Noun Phrase, and PP is for Prepositional Phrase. The syntactic depth of this tree is 5, and the Syntactic links span is equal to $10/7 = 1.43$. For example, the determiner 'the' is related to 'congress' and not 'US.' Therefore, this particular link covers a distance of 2 words. Based on Mothe and Tangui (40).

The features extracted from the query included morphological features such as the average number of morphemes per query word. A morpheme is a primary linguistic unit that has semantic meaning, and words with many morphemes are known to be more difficult to match with morphologically similar words. Other morphological features used were the number of proper nouns in the query and, similarly, the number of acronyms, numeral values, unknown tokens, etc.

Syntactical features of the query were extracted by a shallow parser. The parser analyzes the query raw text to construct a parse tree that identifies syntactic relations between the words based on grammatical rules. Features extracted from the parse tree include the depth of the tree, which is a measure of syntactic complexity, and the syntactic link span which relates to the average distance between query words in the tree. Figure 4.1 displays the syntactic tree for TREC topic 158: *"Term limitations for members of the US congress"*.

Another linguistic feature studied by Mothe and Tanguy was the polysemy value which is the average number of synsets per word in the WordNet dictionary. A synset is a set of synonyms defined by Wordnet, and a word can belong to several different synsets. This value roughly corresponds to the different semantic meanings a given word can have.

The main (negative) result of that study was that most linguistic features do not correlate well with the system performance. Only the syntactic links span and the polysemy value were shown to have some (low) correlation. Similar negative results were reported by Hauff (21) who tested the "average semantic distance" of the query terms for performance prediction. The semantic distance between two terms is the minimal path length between the two corresponding synsets of these terms in the WordNet taxonomy, and the average semantic distance is the average distance between all pairs of query terms. The prediction quality was low, and it varied over the benchmarks used for testing. This is quite surprising as intuitively poor performance can be expected for ambiguous queries. Apparently, term ambiguity should be rather measured using corpus-based approaches, since a term that might be ambiguous with respect to the general vocabulary, may have only a single interpretation in the corpus. Though, the existing (even low) correlation indicates a potential of a link between linguistic characteristics of the query text and the query difficulty.

4.2   STATISTICAL APPROACHES

Statistical pre-retrieval predictors for query difficulty were studied extensively (25; 27; 68; 23) and a comprehensive evaluation of their performance can be found in (21).

4.2.1   DEFINITIONS

Most of the statistical-based prediction methods are based on analyzing the distribution of the query term frequencies within the collection. Two term statistics that are frequently used are the inverse document frequency (*idf*) and the inverse collection term frequency (*ictf*) (34) of the query terms. Both statistics are popular measures for the relative importance of the query terms and are usually measured by the following formulas:

$$idf(t) = \log\left(\frac{N}{N_t}\right)$$

where N is the number of documents in the collection and N_t is the number of documents containing the term t. Similarly, the inverse collection term frequency is measure by

$$ictf(t) = \log\left(\frac{|D|}{tf(t, D)}\right)$$

where $|D|$ is the number of all terms in collection D, and $tf(t, D)$ is the term frequency (number of occurrences) of term t in D.

Several pre-retrieval predictors are based on estimation of the probability of selecting a query term from the query and from the collection. These probabilities are usually approximated by maximum likelihood estimation

$$Pr(t|q) \overset{def}{=} \frac{tf(t, q)}{|q|}$$

where $tf(t, q)$ is the term frequency of term t in query q, and $|q|$ is the number of terms in q.

Similarly, the probability of selecting a term from the collection is approximated by

$$Pr(t|D) \overset{def}{=} \frac{tf(t, D)}{|D|}.$$

Statistical predictors can be categorized into four main categories, according to the query characteristics which they try to estimate: 1) specificity of the query, i.e., how specific the query expression is; 2) similarity of the query to the collection; 3) coherence of the query term distribution; and 4) the relationship strength between the query terms. In the following, we describe these four categories.

4.2.2   SPECIFICITY

The specificity of the query is reflected by the query terms' distribution over the collection. In general, a query composed of common non-specific terms is deemed to be more difficult to answer. For example, consider the TREC topic 531 *"who and whom"*. Such a query is composed of only frequent non-specific terms thus finding relevant documents for it is hard.

The *query scope (QS)* predictor, suggested by He and Ounis (25), measures the percentage of documents containing at least one of the query terms in the collection. High query scope indicates many candidates for retrieval thus separating relevant results from non-relevant results might be more difficult. Note that the query scope of the *"who and whom"* query is expected to be very high. The query scope has marginal prediction quality for short queries only, while for long queries its quality drops significantly (25)[1].

Several pre-retrieval predictors were suggested based on the query term statistics, assuming that the distribution of those values is an intrinsic feature that affects the retrieval performance. The *avgIDF* and the *avgICTF* predictors measure the average of the *idf* and *ictf* values of the query terms (42). The assumption is that queries with high average value, i.e., queries composed of infrequent terms, are easier to satisfy. Other variants measure the maximal value among the query terms, (*maxIDF, maxICTF*). The *varIDF, varICTF* predictors measure the variance of those values, assuming that low variance reflects the non-existence of dominant terms in the query, and therefore may affect the quality of results. These predictors indeed show some correlation with the system performance (25; 42).

Inspired by the post-retrieval *Clarity* predictor, which will be introduced in Chapter 5, the *simplified clarity score* $(SCS(q))$ (25) measures the Kullback-Leibler divergence of the (simplified) query language model from the collection language model, as an indication for query specificity.

The KL-divergence between the query q and the collection D is computed as follows:

$$SCS(q) = \sum_{t \in q} Pr(t|q) \log \left(\frac{Pr(t|q)}{Pr(t|D)} \right).$$

It is easy to show that SCS is strongly related to the $avgICTF$ predictor (21), assuming each term appears only once in the query (a reasonable assumption for short queries). In such a case, $SCS(q) = \log \frac{1}{|q|} + avgICTF(q)$. Thus, SCS measures the specificity of the query while also taking into account the query length.

---

[1] Note that for calculating the query-scope, the dynamic (query dependent) set of documents that contain at least one of the query terms should be enumerated – a process that requires some level of retrieval. Therefore, QS cannot be considered as a "pure" pre-retrieval predictor.

The average based predictors have an intrinsic advantage since they normalize the prediction value by the number of query terms, thus they are more robust to query length and are more plausible to compare the performance of queries of varying lengths. As we will see in the following, some measures for prediction quality are sensitive to the query length, therefore, are non-robust while measured over different sets of queries.

4.2.3   SIMILARITY

Alternative pre-retrieval predictors measure the similarity between the query and the collection. The main argument behind this approach is that queries that are similar to the collection are easier to answer since high similarity potentially indicates the existence of many relevant documents to the query.

Zhao et al. (68) measure the vector-space based query similarity to the collection, while considering the collection as a one large document composed of concatenation of all the documents. The *collection query similarity* of a query term is defined as follows:

$$SCQ(t) = (1 + \log(tf(t, D))) \cdot idf(t)$$

Three predictors that are based on this measure were suggested and evaluated by the same authors (68). The *sumSCQ* predictor sums the SCQ values for all query terms. The *maxSCQ* returns the maximum collection query similarity over all query terms, $maxSCQ(q) = \max_{t \in q} SCQ(t)$, while *avgSCQ* returns the average over query terms, $avgSCQ(q) = \frac{1}{|q|} \sum_{t \in q} SCQ(t)$. In some experiments on TREC benchmarks (68), the query similarity based predictors perform reasonably well, compared to other pre-retrieval predictors.

4.2.4   COHERENCY

He et al. (27) investigated the potential of query-coherence-based measures to predict query difficulty. The query coherence with this respect is related to the inter-similarity of documents containing the query terms. The new-class of pre-retrieval predictors that measure coherency rely on heavy analysis during indexing time, in order to be exploited during search. Each term in the index vocabulary is associated with a coherence score, $CS(t)$, which reflects the average pairwise similarity between all pairs of documents in D_t, the set of documents containing t:

$$CS(t) = \frac{\sum_{(d_i, d_j) \in D_t} sim(d_i, d_j)}{|D_t|(|D_t| - 1)},$$

where $sim(d_i, d_j)$ is the cosine similarity between the two vector-space representations of the documents. The query coherence score is the average coherence scores of its terms.

The coherence predictor, also computed at indexing time, requires a great amount of computation in order to construct a pointwise similarity matrix for all pair of documents in the index. An alternative less expensive approach, suggested by Zhao et al. (68), measures $VAR(t)$, the variance of the term weights over the documents containing it in the collection. The weight of a term that occurs in a document is determined by the specific retrieval approach. For example, $w(t, d) = \frac{\log(1 + tf(t,d)) \cdot idf(t)}{|d|}$ (10), is a popular *tf-idf* based ranking implementation.

Intuitively, if the variance of the term weight distribution over D_t is low, then the retrieval system will be less able to differentiate between highly relevant and less relevant documents, and the query is, therefore, likely to be more difficult. Note that the term variance $Var(t)$ can be computed at indexing time thus the summation, the maximum, or the average values of the query terms can be calculated prior to the retrieval process. *maxVAR* and *avgVAR* are the maximum value and the average value of $Var(t)$ over all query terms, respectively. These predictors outperformed the CS predictor in a comparison study performed over several TREC benchmarks (23).

4.2.5   TERM RELATEDNESS

Term relatedness based predictors explore term co-occurrence statistics. They predict good performance if the query terms co-occur frequently in the collection, assuming all query terms are related to the same topic. For example, the query *"high blood pressure"* is expected to be "easy" as evidently the query terms frequently co-occur in the corpus.

The *pointwise mutual information (PMI)* is a popular measure of co-occurrence statistics of two terms in the collection,

$$PMI(t_1, t_2) = \log \frac{Pr(t_1, t_2 | D)}{Pr(t_1 | D) Pr(t_2 | D)},$$

where $Pr(t_1, t_2 | D)$ is the probability of the two terms to co-occur in the corpus, which can be approximated by maximum likelihood estimation. Such an estimation requires efficient tools for gathering collocation statistics from the corpus, to allow dynamic usage at query run-time.

The predictors *avgPMI(q)* and *maxPMI(q)* (21) measure the average and the maximum PMI over all pairs of terms in the query, respectively. Note that high average PMI value indicates a query with strongly related terms. Such a query will probably be best served by retrieval methods that consider term proximity (38).

4.3   EVALUATING PRE-RETRIEVAL METHODS

Many works evaluated the prediction quality of pre-retrieval prediction methods (25; 42; 68; 27; 23); however, each study employed its own search engine over different datasets and queries, thus results cannot be compared on the same scale.

Lately, Hauff (21) compared the prediction quality of various pre-retrieval methods over several TREC collections and topics, using the same retrieval method, thus all prediction results are comparable. The retrieval method used by all predictors was the query likelihood language model with Dirichlet smoothing (67), as provided by the open-source Lemur toolkit (*www.lemurproject.org*). In all experiments, the retrieval parameters were fixed to the same values, so prediction quality of the different predictors could be compared[2].

---

[2]Hauff (21) also experimented with several other retrieval methods.

Table 4.1 shows the attributes of the TREC collections used in this study, and the set of TREC topics the predictors were tested on. The ROBUST collection is a collection of news articles. WT10G is a collection of web pages, and GOV2 is a collection of pages extracted from some *.gov* domains. For all collections, queries were derived from the TREC topic titles. These collections were previously used by most query-performance-prediction studies (64; 12; 70; 56; 69; 16; 48).

Table 4.1: Attributes of the TREC collections used for prediction quality estimation (21).

Collection	Data source	Number of documents	TREC topic numbers	Avg. number of relevant docs per topic
ROBUST	Disk 4&5-CR	528,155	301-450	69
WT10G	WT10g	1,692,095	451-550	61
GOV2	GOV2	25,205,179	701-850	181

The query performance prediction methods compared were the following:

1. Average inverse document frequency of query terms (*avgIDF*) (25)

2. Simplified Clarity score (*SCS*) (25)

3. Maximum (over query terms) of Collection query similarity (*maxSCQ*) (68)

4. Maximum variance of the query term weights distribution (*maxVAR*) (68)

5. Average pointwise mutual information (*avgPMI*) (21)

Tables 4.2 and 4.3 show the linear and the rank correlation of actual AP and predicted AP, for those predictors, over the queries test sets.

Table 4.2: Comparison of various pre-retrieval prediction methods using Pearson correlation. The results of the top two predictors, for each query set column, are boldfaced. From (21).

	ROBUST			WT10G		GOV2		
	301-350	351-400	401-450	451-500	501-550	701-750	751-800	801-850
avgIDF	**0.591**	0.374	**0.576**	0.153	0.221	0.393	0.315	0.172
SCS	**0.578**	0.319	0.518	0.087	0.189	0.325	0.278	0.096
maxSCQ	0.122	**0.507**	0.524	**0.429**	**0.393**	**0.473**	0.371	**0.306**
maxVAR	0.369	**0.445**	**0.764**	**0.381**	**0.533**	**0.435**	**0.434**	**0.345**
avgPMI	0.316	0.376	0.438	0.288	0.235	0.431	**0.456**	0.037

The correlation results reveal that *maxVAR* and *maxSCQ* dominant the rest of predictors, and they are most stable over the collections and query sets. The prediction quality of *maxSCQ* is comparable to *maxVAR*; however, its performance significantly drops for one of the queries sets (301-350), thus it is less robust. Another interesting observation is that prediction is harder on the Web collections (WT10G and GOV2) compared to the news collection, probably due to higher heterogeneity of the data.

Table 4.3: Comparison of various pre-retrieval prediction methods using $Kendall's\text{-}\tau$ correlation. The results of the top two predictors, for each query set column, are boldfaced. From (21).

	ROBUST			WT10G			GOV2	
	301-350	351-400	401-450	451-500	501-550	701-750	751-800	801-850
avgIDF	**0.314**	0.271	0.313	0.249	0.187	0.277	0.253	0.160
SCS	0.286	0.227	0.277	0.174	0.136	0.211	0.240	0.095
maxSCQ	0.181	**0.422**	**0.474**	**0.435**	**0.270**	**0.331**	0.291	**0.209**
maxVAR	**0.353**	**0.434**	**0.494**	**0.339**	**0.327**	0.288	**0.318**	**0.243**
avgPMI	0.176	0.290	0.232	0.208	0.212	**0.301**	**0.314**	0.034

4.4 SUMMARY

In this chapter, we covered leading pre-retrieval performance prediction methods that measure linguistic and statistical features of the query in order to identify hidden attributes that may affect the quality of search results. Despite the inferiority of the pre-retrieval prediction approaches, which are not exposed to the actual search results, the experimental results over several TREC benchmarks reveal that some of these predictors perform reasonably well, and as we shall see in the next chapter, their prediction quality is comparable to that of more complex post-retrieval prediction methods.

CHAPTER 5

Post-Retrieval Prediction Methods

So far, we have discussed pre-retrieval prediction methods that only consider the query for prediction, by analyzing the query statistical and linguistic characteristics. In contrast, post-retrieval methods analyze the search results, that is, the list of documents most highly ranked in response to the query. Therefore, post-retrieval methods are usually more complex as the top-results are retrieved and analyzed. Moreover, in contrast to pre-retrieval methods, the prediction quality of post-retrieval methods strongly depends on the retrieval process, as different results are expected for the same query when using different retrieval methods.

However, if we ignore the search results as pre-retrieval methods do, we risk missing important aspects of the query difficulty as reflected by the results exposed to the users. In extreme cases, pre-retrieval methods might wrongly judge a query as "easy", even in cases that the retrieved results are totally irrelevant, due to flaws or failures in the retrieval process. Moreover, query independent factors such as document (static) scores (authority, freshness, etc), have strong effect on the ranking of search results but can hardly be predicted a priori. In addition, the coherence of the search results, i.e., how focused they are on aspects related to the query, is not captured by the query text and is hard to predict without a deep analysis of the result list.

Furthermore, as the complexity of retrieval methods increases, the quality of search results is affected by many more factors that are query-independent. Modern search engines consider personalization and geospatial aspects of the searcher, the diversity of results, trends as reflected by query log analysis, and many other factors. Such considerations cannot be predicted by analyzing the query only; however, they strongly affect the search results.

Therefore, post-retrieval prediction methods are still considered attractive and dominant, despite their higher complexity, and retain most of the attention of the IR community. New methods are still proposed and on-going comprehensive research on post-retrieval methods is still being published in leading conferences and journals.

Post-retrieval methods can be categorized into three main paradigms. *Clarity* based methods directly measure the "focus" (clarity) of the search results with respect to the corpus. Robustness-based methods evaluate how robust the results are to perturbations in the query, the result list, and the retrieval method. Score distribution based methods analyze the score distribution of the search result as an indicator of query difficulty. The following sections discuss these three prominent paradigms.

5.1   *CLARITY*

The *Clarity* approach for performance prediction (14) is based on measuring the "coherence" (clarity) of the result-list *with respect* to the corpus. We expect good results to be focused on the query's topic; thus, a shared vocabulary of words related to the topic is expected to be found in those results.

According to the *Clarity* approach, "coherence" is the extent to which top results use the same language. Specifically, *Clarity* considers the discrepancy between the likelihood of words most frequently used in retrieved documents to their likelihood in the whole corpus. The conjecture is that a common language of the retrieved documents, which is distinct from general language of the whole corpus is an indication for good results. In contrast, in an unfocused set of results, the language of retrieved documents tends to be more similar to the general language, and retrieval is expected to be less effective.

5.1.1   DEFINITION

Let q, d, and D denote a query, a document and a collection of documents, respectively. Let $D_q \subseteq D$ denotes the result set for q. The *Clarity* measure applied by Cronen-Townsend et al. (14) is based on measuring the KL-divergence between the language model of the result set, $Pr(\cdot|D_q)$, and the language model of the entire collection, $Pr(\cdot|D)$, as given by Equation 5.1.

$$Clarity(q) = KL_{div}(Pr(\cdot|D_q)||Pr(\cdot|D)) = \sum_{t \in V(D)} Pr(t|D_q) \log \frac{Pr(t|D_q)}{Pr(t|D)} \qquad (5.1)$$

where $V(D)$ is the vocabulary (the set of unique terms) of the collection.

Clarity(q) measures the divergence between two language models: $Pr(\cdot|D_q)$, which is the probability distribution over the terms in the result set D_q; and $Pr(\cdot|D)$, which is the probability distribution over the terms in the collection D. We describe the language modeling approach used by Cronen-Townsend et al. (14) to infer those distributions from the raw data.

The language model induced from the corpus is estimated directly, based on the maximum likelihood estimation (MLE), using the relative frequency of the term occurrences in the collection, $Pr(t|D) \stackrel{def}{=} \frac{tf(t,D)}{|D|}$.

The language model induced from the result set is computed by summing over all documents in the list:

$$Pr(t|D_q) \stackrel{def}{=} \sum_{d \in D_q} Pr(t|d)Pr(d|q).$$

The probability of term t in document d is estimated by the relative frequency of t in d, smoothed by a linear combination with its collection relative frequency:

$$Pr(t|d) \stackrel{def}{=} \lambda \frac{tf(t,d)}{|d|} + (1 - \lambda)Pr(t|D)$$

where λ might be a free parameter (Jelinek-Mercer smoothing) or document dependent (Dirichlet smoothing: $\lambda = \frac{|d|}{\mu + |d|}$, where μ is a free parameter (35)).

The probability of a document given the query $Pr(d|q)$ is obtained by Bayesian inversion, with uniform prior probabilities for documents in D_q and zero prior probability for all documents not in D_q,

$$Pr(d|q) \stackrel{def}{=} \frac{Pr(q|d)Pr(d)}{\sum_{d' \in D_q} Pr(q|d')Pr(d')} \propto Pr(q|d);$$

$Pr(q|d)$, the likelihood of a query given a document, is estimated using the query-likelihood based (unigram) language modeling approach (50)

$$Pr(q|d) \stackrel{def}{=} \prod_{t \in q} Pr(t|d).$$

The efficiency of *Clarity* score computation by Equation 5.1 is dominated by the estimation of the language model of the result set, since the collection's language model can be precomputed at indexing time. The main difficulty is the requirement to sum over all documents in the result set. This sum can be approximated by considering only top documents in the list or by sampling techniques. In the original work of Cronen-Townsend et al. (14), the language model of the result set was estimated by Monte-Carlo sampling from the result set until a limit of 500 unique documents is reached. In a later work of the same authors (15), the top 500 documents in the result set were analyzed, following the observation that $Pr(d|q)$ falls off sharply below this cutoff. The sensitivity of *Clarity*, as well as other post-retrieval predictors, to the number of top results used for performance prediction is further discussed in Section 5.5.

5.1.2 EXAMPLES

The following example was first given in (14). Consider the following two TREC queries, *"What adjustments should be made once federal action occurs?"*, and *"Show me any predictions for changes in the prime lending rate and any changes made in the prime lending rates"*. These queries happen to be two query variants for TREC topic 56 from the TREC-9 query track (8). In this track, each topic was presented by two variant queries; one (less coherent) query is formulated based on the topic only, and one (more coherent) query that is formulated based on the topic and some given relevant documents. In the example above, the first query is the topic-based query which is expected to be less coherent than the second one which was formulated after considering some relevant documents to the topic.

The *Clarity* of the two query variants is plotted in Figure 5.1. The *Clarity* score of the top 40 contributing terms, sorted in descending order of contribution to the query accumulated *Clarity* score. In this representation, the *Clarity* score is the total area under the graph, leading to a *Clarity* score of 2.85 for the first (coherent) query and 0.37 for the second (less coherent) query. The contrast between the high-*Clarity* query and the low-*Clarity* query is clear.

Another instructive illustration for the *Clarity* prediction power was given in (21). Figure 5.2 shows the *Clarity* scores of some TREC topics for three different result sets. For each topic, the

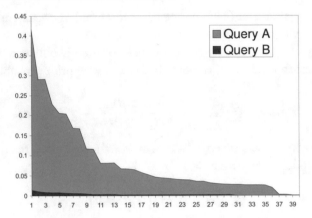

Figure 5.1: Clear (A) versus vague (B) query. The horizontal axis denotes the most significant contributing terms and the vertical axis the contribution of each term to the clarity score. Based on (14).

figure plots the *Clarity* score of 1) the set of relevant documents, 2) a sampled set of non-relevant documents[1], and 3) a random sample of documents from the collection. As expected, the *Clarity* score of the relevant set is higher, in general, than the scores of the non-relevant and the random sets. It is interesting to note that the *Clarity* score of the non-relevant document set is usually higher than the score of the random set, as the latter one should be low (by definition).

5.1.3   OTHER *CLARITY* MEASURES

The *Clarity* measure was the first predictor proposed for query difficulty and can still be considered as state-of-the-art. Inspired by the success of the *Clarity* score, different forms of *Clarity* estimation were proposed. Amati et al. (1) applied a similar approach by measuring the divergence between query terms' frequency in the result list and that in the entire corpus, following the *divergence from randomness framework*. The Jensen-Shannon divergence (JSD) between the result set and the entire corpus has also been shown to indicate query difficulty (12). The JSD is a symmetrized and smoothed version of the Kullback-Leibler divergence. Carmel et al. (12) validated that query difficulty is correlated with the JSD distances between the query q, the relevant documents set, R_q, and the collection D. In the absence of knowledge about R_q, this set can be approximated by finding a document subset from the result set D_q, that leads to a shorter distance to the query. The distances are then combined to provide a prediction of query difficulty.

Cronen-Townsend et al. (15), in a later work, applied a weighted KL-divergence measure which considers the document ranking while constructing the language model of the result set. A variant of *Clarity* which utilizes only documents containing all query terms and ignores high-

---

[1]The Qrels sets in TREC contain many documents that were retrieved by participants, but they were judged as non-relevant to the topic. Therefore, these non-relevant documents exhibit some similarity to the query. The non-relevant set was created by random sampling from those documents.

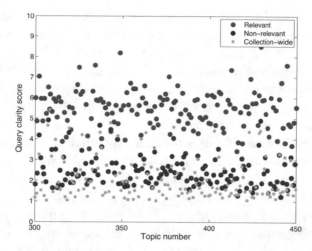

Figure 5.2: The *Clarity* score of some TREC topics for 1) a set of relevant documents, 2) a sampled set of non-relevant documents, and 3) a random sample of documents. Based on (21).

frequency terms in the language models was proposed for improving *Clarity* estimation on the Web (24).

5.2   ROBUSTNESS

An alternative effective performance-prediction paradigm is based on estimating the robustness of the result set. Robustness can be measured with respect to perturbations in the query, in the documents, and in the retrieval method. Intuitively, the more robust the result list is, the less difficult the query. In the following, we cover these three types of robustness.

5.2.1   QUERY PERTURBATION

Methods based on query perturbation measure the robustness of the result list to small modifications of the query. When small changes to the query result in large changes to the search results, our confidence in the correctness of these results is diminished.

Zhou and Croft (71) proposed a framework for measuring query robustness, named *Query Feedback (QF)*, which models retrieval as a communication channel problem. The input is the query, the channel is the search system, and the set of results is the noisy output of the channel. From the list of results a new query is generated, based on the terms with maximum contribution to the *Clarity* score, and then a second list of results is retrieved for that query. The overlap between the two lists is used as a robustness score. When the overlap between the two result sets is lower, the noise in the communication channel in higher; hence, the query is more difficult.

The assumption behind the QF predictor is that the language model induced from the result set is an approximation of the "true" query language model that generates both the original query and results. Therefore, we anticipate that the results for a query that is based on that language model will be similar to the original results, and dissimilarity may indicate query difficulty.

Query perturbation was also examined by Vinay et al. (56), who studied the effect of small modifications to the query term weights on the search results. Similarly, if results were changed drastically then the query is presumed to be difficult.

Another type of robustness with respect to the query perturbation was measured by the overlap between the result set retrieved in response to the entire query and the result sets retrieved in response to sub-queries composed of individual query terms (65). This was done following the observation that some query terms have little or no influence on the retrieved documents, especially in difficult queries. The *overlap* between the results returned in response to the full query and a sub-query (that is, a query based on a single query term) is measured as the size of intersection between the top ten results of the two queries. The overlaps between the query and all sub-queries are represented by a histogram $h(i), i = 0, 1, ..., 10$, where entry $h(i)$ counts the number of sub-queries that agree with the full query for exactly i documents in the top 10 results. This histogram represents the agreement between the query to its sub-queries and is closely related to the κ-statistics (65), which is a standard measure for the strength of agreement between experts.

Figure 5.3 illustrates a typical histogram for a difficult query and an easy query. The figure shows the average histogram for all difficult queries in a training set of 250 queries (P@10 $\leq$ 0.3) and the average histogram for the easy queries (P@10 $\geq$ 0.5). Queries that perform poorly have their overlaps clustered in the lower area of the histogram and vice versa. This suggests that a good pattern for estimating query difficulty would be one where the query is not dominated by a single keyword. Rather, all (or at least most) keywords contribute somewhat to the final results.

One of the advantages of the overlap estimator is the search engine's ability to apply it efficiently during query execution since all data it uses can be generated by the search engine during its normal mode of operation. The top results for each of the sub-queries can be accumulated simultaneously during evaluation of the full query.

5.2.2   DOCUMENT PERTURBATION

The effect of document perturbations on the resultant retrieved list is another form of robustness estimation (56; 70). The top results are injected with noise (e.g., by adding or removing terms) and then re-ranked. High similarity between the original list and the re-ranked list reveals query robustness. The reason is that small *random* perturbations of documents are unlikely to result in major changes to documents' retrieval scores. Thus, if the retrieval-scores of documents in the result set are spread over a wide range, then these perturbations are unlikely to result in significant changes to the ranking. Consequently, the list could be considered as robust with respect to documents' perturbations.

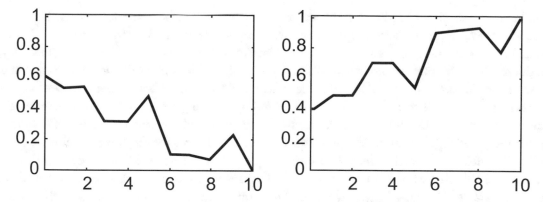

Figure 5.3: A typical histogram of overlaps for difficult queries (left) and for easy queries (right). The horizontal axis measures the amount of document overlap and the vertical the fraction of query terms with this overlap. From (65).

5.2.3 RETRIEVAL PERTURBATION

In general, different retrieval methods retrieve different results for the same query, when applied over the same document collection. Therefore, a high overlap in results retrieved by different methods may be related to high agreement on the (usually sparse) set of relevant results for the query. In contrast, low overlap may indicate no agreement on the relevant results, hence, query difficulty.

Aslam and Pavlu (2) studied robustness of the query with respect to using different retrieval methods. Specifically, they showed that the disagreement between result lists returned for the query by multiple scoring functions is an indication for query difficulty. Therefore, query difficulty is predicted by submitting the query to different retrieval methods and measuring the diversity of the ranked lists obtained. To measure the diversity of a set of ranked lists, each ranking is mapped to a distribution over the document collection, where highly ranked documents are associated with higher distribution weights, and vice versa. Given the set of distributions, the JSD distance is used to measure the diversity of the distributions corresponding to these ranked lists.

Experimental results on TREC data show a relatively high correlation between systems agreement and query performance. By analyzing the submissions of all participants to several TREC tracks, Aslam and Pavlu showed that the agreement between submissions highly correlates with the query difficulty, as measured by the median performance (AP) of all participants. Moreover, as the JSD between more submissions is analyzed, the prediction quality improves.

5.2.4 COHESION

The cohesion of the result set, another aspect of robustness, can be measured by its clustering patterns, and relates to query difficulty (56). Following the "cluster hypothesis" (54), which states that documents relevant to a given query are likely to be similar to one another, the lack of "clear" clusters in the result set implies that the list does not contain many relevant documents. Therefore, a good retrieval returns a single, tight cluster, while a poorly performing retrieval returns a loosely related set of documents covering many topics. Vinay et al. (56) measured the "clustering tendency" of the result set by the distance between a randomly selected document and it's nearest neighbor from the result set. When the list contains inherent clusters, the distance between the random document and its closest neighbor, d_{nn}, is likely to be much larger than the distance between d_{nn} and its own nearest neighbor in the list. This measure corresponds to using the Cox-Lewis statistic, which measures the "randomness" level of the documents retrieved for the query by the system.

The utilization of the *cluster hypothesis* for query-performance prediction was also demonstrated by Diaz (16) who showed that query performance correlates with the extent to which the result set *respects* the *cluster hypothesis*, that is, the extent to which similar documents receive similar retrieval scores. In contrast, a difficult query might be detected when similar documents are scored differently.

In Diaz's *spatial autocorrelation* approach, a document's "regularized" retrieval-score is the average of the scores of its most similar documents, weighted according to their similarity to the document. Then, the linear correlation of the regularized scores with original scores is used for difficulty estimation. Comprehensive experiments demonstrate that autocorrelation outperforms *Clarity* on several TREC benchmarks. However, as the author noted, there are several cases, e.g., when diversity of results is in favor, that high autocorrelation may indicate a poor performance as we prefer only one representative from a cluster at the top results.

5.3 SCORE DISTRIBUTION ANALYSIS

Measuring the *Clarity* or the robustness of a query requires an analysis of the result set—a time-consuming task in most cases, especially when retrieving the content of the top results. An appealing and less expensive alternative is to analyze the score distribution of the result set to identify query difficulty. The following section describes several predictors that are based on score distribution analysis.

In most retrieval models, the similarity of documents to a query is reflected by their retrieval scores. Hence, the distribution of retrieval scores can potentially help predict query performance. Indeed, the highest retrieval-score and the mean of top scores indicate query performance (53) since, in general, low scores of the top-ranked documents exhibit some difficulty in retrieval. As another example, the difference between retrieval scores produced in a query-independent manner (e.g., based on link analysis) and those produced in a query-dependent way, which reflects the "discriminative power" of the query, was also shown to be an indicator for query performance (6).

A recently proposed predictor is the *Weighted Information Gain* (*WIG*) measure (71). *WIG* essentially measures the divergence between the mean retrieval score of top-ranked documents and that of the entire corpus. The hypothesis is that the more similar these documents are to the query, with respect to the query similarity exhibited by a general non-relevant document (i.e., the corpus), the more effective the retrieval.

WIG was originally proposed and employed in the *MRF retrieval framework* (38), which allows for arbitrary text features to be incorporated into the scoring formula, in particular features that are based on occurrences of single terms, ordered phrases, and unordered phrases. However, if no term-dependencies are considered – i.e., a bag-of-words representation is used, then MRF reduces to using the query likelihood model. Indeed, it was noted that *WIG* is very effective under such implementation (69).

Specifically, given query q, collection D, a ranked list D_q of documents, and the set of k top-ranked documents, D_q^k, *WIG* is calculated as follows:

$$WIG(q) = \frac{1}{k} \sum_{d \in D_q^k} \sum_{t \in q} \lambda(t) \log \frac{Pr(t|d)}{Pr(t|D)}$$

where $\lambda(t)$ reflects the relative weight of the term's type t and is inversely related to the square root of the number of query terms of that type. For the simplified case when all query terms are simple keywords, this parameter collapses to $\lambda(t) = \frac{1}{\sqrt{|q|}}$, a normalization with respect to the query length, which supports inter-query compatibility.

Another predictor suggested recently that belongs to this score-analysis family of predictors is based on estimating the potential amount of query drift in the list of top-retrieved documents. Work on pseudo-relevance feedback based query expansion often uses a centroid representation of the list D_q^k as an expanded "query model". While using only the centroid yields poor retrieval performance, anchoring it to the query via interpolation yields improved performance, leading to the conclusion that the centroid manifests query drift (39). Thus, the centroid could be viewed as a prototypical "misleader" as it exhibits (some) similarity to the query by virtue of the way it is constructed, but this similarity is dominated by non-query-related aspects that lead to query drift. Shtok et al. (48) showed that μ, the mean score of results in D_q^k, corresponds in several retrieval methods to the retrieval score of a centroid-based representation of D_q^k. Thus, the standard deviation of the retrieval scores in D_q^k, which measures the dispersion of scores around the average, reflects the divergence of results from a non-relevant document that exhibits high query similarity (the centroid).

The Normalized Query Commitment (*NQC*) predictor (48) measures the standard deviation of retrieval scores in D_q^k, normalized by the score of the whole collection $Score(D)$:

$$NQC(q) = \frac{\sqrt{\frac{1}{k} \sum_{d \in D_q^k} (Score(d) - \mu)^2}}{|Score(D)|}.$$

Documents with retrieval scores (much) higher than μ, the score of a prototypical misleader, are potentially less likely to manifest query drift; therefore, high positive divergence from μ of the retrieval scores of these documents correlates with improved retrieval effectiveness. Such documents could be considered as exhibiting positive query commitment. For documents with scores lower than μ, if we assume that there are only a few relevant documents in the corpus that yield "reasonable" query similarity, then a small overall number of documents exhibiting query similarity can potentially indicate a small number of misleaders. The lower the retrieval score of a document with respect to μ, the less it exhibits reasonable query similarity. Hence, the overall number of misleaders in D_q^k decreases with increased negative divergence from μ. As a consequence, high standard deviation correlates with lower query drift of D_q^k and hence with better query performance.

Figure 5.4 shows a geometric interpretation of NQC. The two top graphs present retrieval scores curves for the top 100 results for "difficult" and "easy" queries, respectively. The shift between these two scenarios, which is further exemplified in the bottom graph, amounts to rotating (and curving) the retrieval scores line in a clockwise manner. The extent of the rotation is measured by NQC.

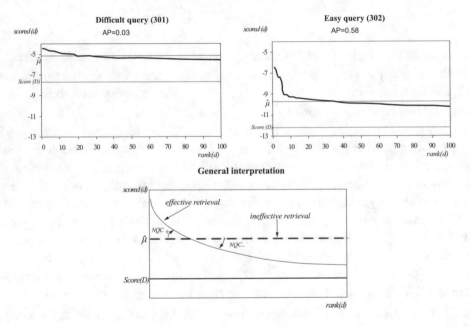

Figure 5.4: Geometric interpretation of NQC. The top two graphs present retrieval-scores curves for "difficult" and "easy" queries. The shift between these two scenarios, which is further exemplified in the bottom graph, amounts to rotating (and curving) the retrieval-scores line in a clockwise manner. The extent of the rotation is measured by NQC. From Shtok et al. (48).

NQC analyzes the score distribution of the top results similarly to WIG. In contrast to WIG, this estimator measures the divergence of results from the centroid, a "pseudo non-relevant document" that exhibits a relatively high query similarity, as reflected by the standard deviation of the score distribution. WIG, in contrast, measures the dispersion of the top results' scores from the whole collection, a non-relevant pseudo document that is not necessarily similar to the query. The high "predictive power" of both NQC and WIG over several benchmarks, as well as their computational efficiency, reflects the suitability of score distribution analysis for query performance prediction.

Table 5.1: Test collections and topics. The last column reports the average number of relevant documents per topic. From (49).

Collection	Data source	Number of documents	TREC topic numbers	Avg. number of rel. docs per topic
TREC4	Disks 2&3	567,529	201-250	130
TREC5	Disks 2&4	524,929	251-300	110
ROBUST	Disk 4&5-CR	528,155	301-450,601-700	69
WT10G	WT10g	1,692,095	451-550	61
GOV2	GOV2	25,205,179	701-850	181

Table 5.2: The prediction quality (Pearson correlation) of post-retrieval predictors. The two best results in a column are boldfaced. From (49).

Predictor	TREC4	TREC5	WT10G	ROBUST	GOV2
Clarity	0.453	**0.42**	0.348	0.512	0.433
WIG	0.544	0.297	0.376	**0.543**	**0.479**
NQC	**0.588**	0.354	**0.488**	**0.566**	0.36
QF	**0.627**	**0.414**	0.426	0.285 ·	**0.476**

5.4   EVALUATING POST-RETRIEVAL METHODS

Similarly, to the evaluation of pre-retrieval predictors, there are many works that study the prediction quality of post-retrieval predictors (12; 71; 16; 48). However, to provide a coherent comparison picture we should measure the prediction quality of different predictors on the same scale, using the same datasets, the same sets of queries, and the same retrieval methods. Shtok et al. (49) conducted such an experiment on the TREC collections, summarized in Table 5.1.

In these experiments, the authors used the TREC topic titles for queries, except for TREC4 for which no titles are provided, and hence, topic descriptions are used. They applied tokenization, Porter-stemming, and stopword removal (using the INQUERY list) to all data via the Lemur toolkit (*www.lemurproject.org*). The query likelihood language model with Dirichlet smoothing was used for retrieval (67).

The post-retrieval predictors compared in this experiment were *Clarity* (14), *WIG* (71), *NQC* (48) and query feedback (*QF*) (71). Recall that *Clarity* measures the KL divergence between a (language) model induced from the result-list and the corpus model. The *WIG* predictor measures the divergence of retrieval scores of the top-ranked results from that of the corpus. *NQC* measures the normalized standard deviation of the top scores, and *QF* measures the divergence between the original top results for the query and the results obtained for a query constructed from the top results. The number of documents in the result-list was set to 100 for *NQC*, *Clarity* and the *QF* predictors. For *WIG*, this number was set to five following previous recommendations (69).

Table 5.2 shows the Pearson correlation between the actual and predicted AP obtained by the predictors over those datasets. Table 5.3 shows the *Kendall's-τ* correlation. Similarly, to the experimental results with the pre-retrieval methods, there is no clear "winner". All predictors exhibit comparable results. *NQC* exhibits good performance over most collections but does not perform

Table 5.3: The prediction quality ($Kendall's$-τ correlation) of post-retrieval predictors. The two best results in a column are boldfaced. From (49).

Predictor	TREC4	TREC5	WT10G	ROBUST	GOV2
Clarity	0.352	0.296	0.291	**0.403**	0.293
WIG	**0.491**	0.252	**0.300**	0.386	**0.336**
NQC	0.451	**0.318**	**0.292**	**0.413**	0.231
QF	**0.475**	**0.400**	0.273	0.261	**0.306**

very well on the GOV2 collection. Similarly, *QF* performs well over some of the collections but is inferior to other predictors on the ROBUST collection.

5.5 PREDICTION SENSITIVITY

The prediction quality of all post-retrieval predictors discussed so far depend on several configuration parameters, especially on the number of top results used for analysis. We question the sensitivity of the predictors to these parameters.

Figure 5.5 presents the results of some experiments with the sensitivity of various predictors. The figure plots the prediction quality (measured by Pearson correlation) of *Clarity*, *WIG*, and *NQC* predictors, over four TREC collections, as a function of the result-list size.

The first observation is that the prediction quality of *Clarity* is robust, with respect to the number of top results used for the language model construction, over all collections. This is due to the fact that the language model constructed from top results weights the documents by their query likelihood retrieval scores. Hence, low-scored documents have little effect on the constructed model and, consequently, on the resultant *Clarity* values.

In contrast, the prediction quality of both *WIG* and *NQC* is sensitive to the number of results. This finding could potentially be attributed to the fact that both measures calculate their prediction based on score-distribution analysis. Specifically, for all collections, *WIG* prediction quality is optimal for low values of retrieved results (often 5), which corresponds to previous findings (71); *WIG* prediction quality significantly drops when we increase the number of results used for calculation. The prediction quality of *NQC* is usually optimal for 80, and then it gradually drops and levels off for higher values[2]. We note, however, that no single predictor of the three dominates the others over the entire tested range of number of retrieved results.

5.6 SUMMARY

In this chapter, we covered post-retrieval prediction methods that analyze the search results while looking for clues for retrieval quality. *Clarity* based approaches measure the coherence of search results

---

[2]In a later work Shtok et al. (49) showed that *NQC* is sensitive to the average number of relevant documents per topic in the collection. For GOV2, which has high such value, *NQC* prediction quality improves with the number of top results used for calculation.

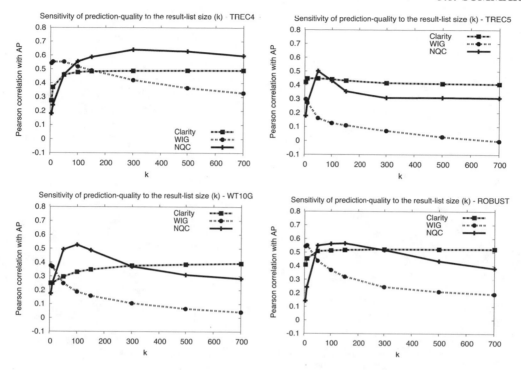

Figure 5.5: Prediction quality (measured by Pearson correlation) of *Clarity*, *WIG*, and *NQC*, over four TREC collections, as a function of the result-list size.

as reflected by their divergence from the whole collection. Robustness-based approaches measure the robustness of results in the presence of perturbations in the query, the document content, and the retrieval method. Score analysis based approaches analyze the score distribution of results. The experimental results with prediction quality over some TREC benchmarks showed comparable performance between leading methods of all types.

The post-retrieval methods described in this chapter are very different in nature as each prediction type focuses on analyzing another aspect of the search results. Therefore, combining several predictors of different types may bring some merit to prediction quality. Similarly, it seems that there is also potential for combining pre-retrieval methods with post-retrieval ones. In the next chapter, we discuss how different predictors can be combined to provide better performance prediction.

CHAPTER 6

Combining Predictors

6.1   LINEAR REGRESSION

The performance predictors described so far measure different aspects of the query; thus, a question arises whether combining these predictors can enhance prediction quality. Many works in the machine learning domain have shown that combining individual classifiers is an effective technique for improving accuracy of classification (30). The basic idea is that a group of experts tends to classify better than a single expert. Similarly, it can be assumed that better performance could be expected as each predictor of the group would have advantages under different circumstances. In other words, if an individual predictor makes a mistake, the others may be able to correct it.

One possible approach for prediction combination uses linear regression based on training data. Given a set of n training queries, each associated with known AP, and a vector of p predicted values given by different predictors, we can learn a weight vector $\bar{\beta}$ that associates a relative weight for each predictor based on its relative contribution to the combined prediction. A linear regression model assumes that the relationship between $AP(q)$ and the p-vector of predictions $\bar{x}_i$ is approximately linear. Thus, the model takes the form of n linear equations, for the n training queries:

$$AP(q_i) = \bar{x}_i \bar{\beta} + \epsilon_i, \; i = 1, \ldots, n$$

where $\bar{x}_i \bar{\beta}$ is the inner-product between vectors $\bar{x}_i$ and $\bar{\beta}$, and ϵ_i is an unobserved random variable, normally distributed, that adds noise to the linear relationship. The linear regression task is to find $\bar{\beta}$ that mostly fits the n equations, usually by minimizing the root mean square error (RMSE)

$$RMSE = \sqrt{\frac{1}{n} \sum_i \left(AP(q_i) - \bar{x}_i \bar{\beta} \right)^2}.$$

Linear regression analysis can be applied to quantify the strength of the relationship between $AP(q)$ and the prediction values $\bar{x}_i$, to assess which predictor may have no relationship with $AP(q)$ at all, and to identify which subsets of predictions contain redundant information about $AP(q)$. Thus, once one of them is known, the others are no longer informative.

6.2   COMBINING PRE-RETRIEVAL PREDICTORS

The pre-retrieval prediction methods described in Chapter 4 measure different aspects of the query as an indication of query difficulty. Therefore, such methods are good candidates to combine, which, hopefully, will lead to improved prediction accuracy.

However, before a combination can take place, we carefully investigate how different the predictors really are, as strong dependency between predictors points out that they measure exactly the same aspect of the query. Hauff (21) studied the correlation between various pre-retrieval predictors over several TREC benchmarks. Table 6.1 shows the linear correlation between prediction values of the predictors over queries 301-450 of the TREC ROBUST collection. Similar results were obtained over other benchmarks.

Table 6.1: Pearson correlation between the prediction values of various pre-retrieval predictors for topics 301-450 over the TREC's ROBUST collection. From (21).

	avgIDF	maxIDF	avgICTF	SCS	SumSCQ	QS
avgIDF		0.721	**0.933**	**0.875**	0.155	0.683
maxIDF			0.694	0.651	0.165	0.417
avgICTF				**0.915**	0.138	0.693
SCS					0.053	0.723
SumSCQ						0.076

As expected, the table shows that *avgIDF* is highly correlated with *avgICTF*, as both measure similar term statistics (Pearson correlation of 0.933). The two predictors are also highly correlated with the simplified Clarity score, *SCS* (0.875 and 0.915, respectively) as there is strong dependency between *SCS* and *avgICTF* (see Chapter 4). The correlation between other predictor pairs is much lower. Interestingly, there is relatively substantial correlation between the query scope predictor (*QS*) and all other predictors, excluding *SumSCQ*, which does not correlate with any of the predictors.

The low correlation between *SumSCQ* and all other predictors illustrates the potential of combining it with other predictors. Hauff et al. (22) experimented with combining pre-retrieval predictors in principled way using several variants of linear regression methods. Ideally, a training set of queries should be used for learning a regression model and this model should be tested on a different, independent set of queries. However, due to the very limited query set size, cross-validation was applied by splitting the query set into k partitions. The linear model was tuned on $k - 1$ partitions and the k'th partition was used for testing. This process was repeated and the evaluation is based on averaging the evaluation results for the k partitions. The results show that in terms of Pearson correlation, the combined predictor is better than individual predictors, although it is comparable to the best single predictor in terms of RMSE. It is likely that the main reason for the disagreement between the two evaluation metrics is the fact that the training data is over-represented at the lower end of the average precision values (0.0-0.2) while very few training queries exist in the middle and high range, which in turn leads to deficient RMSE performance of the (combined) predictor.

6.3 COMBINING POST-RETRIEVAL PREDICTORS

Post-retrieval prediction methods can be combined with each other, as well as with pre-retrieval methods, using the same linear regression and by other regression methods. Unfortunately, not much work has been done in this direction. Yom-Tov et al. (64) combined the pre-predictor *avgIDF* with the post-predictor based on an overlap histogram and reported some improvement in prediction quality. Zhou and Croft (71) integrated *WIG* and *QF* using a simple linear combination where the combination weight is learned from the training data set. A similar linear integration was applied by Diaz (16) for incorporating the spatial autocorrelation predictor with *Clarity* and with the document perturbation based predictor (70). In all those trials, the results of the combined predictor were significantly better than the results of the single predictors, suggesting that the single predictors measure orthogonal properties of the retrieved results that relate to query performance.

6.3.1   COMBINING PREDICTORS BASED ON STATISTICAL DECISION THEORY

The successful combination of *WIG* and *QF* (71) and of autocorrelation and *Clarity* (16) demonstrated the high potential in combining independent predictors and led to attempts to develop a general framework for combining post-retrieval predictors in a principled way.

Shtok et al. (49) suggested such a framework based on statistical decision theory. The framework, denoted *UEF* for *utility-estimation-framework*, is inspired by the *risk minimization framework* (35). In *UEF*, the ranked list of results, D_q, could be viewed as a decision made by the retrieval method in response to a query, q, so as to satisfy the user's hidden information need, I_q. The retrieval effectiveness of D_q reflects the *utility* provided to the user by the system, denoted by $U(D_q|I_q)$.

Therefore, the prediction task in this framework is interpreted as the prediction of the utility the user can gain from the retrieved result list D_q. Suppose that there is an oracle that provides us with a *"true"* model of relevance R_{I_q} representing the *"true"* information need. Suppose also that R_{I_q} can be used to re-rank the result list, $\pi(D_q, R_{I_q})$. Then, according to the *probability ranking principle* (45), using R_{I_q} yields a ranking of maximal utility (e.g., all relevant documents are positioned at the highest ranks, and all non-relevant documents are positioned below the relevant documents). Thus, we can use the maximal-utility ranked list to estimate the utility of the given ranked list, based on their "similarity".

$$U(D_q|I_q) \approx Sim(D_q, \pi(D_q, R_{I_q})). \tag{6.1}$$

In practice, we have no explicit knowledge of the underlying information need except for the information in q — nor do we have an oracle to provide us with a model of relevance. Hence, we use estimates that are based on the information in q and in the corpus. Using statistical decision theory principles, we can approximate Equation 6.1 by the expected similarity between the given ranking and the rankings induced by estimates for R_{I_q}:

$$U(D_q|I_q) \approx \int_{\hat{R}_q} Sim(\pi(D_q, \hat{R}_q), D_q) Pr(\hat{R}_q|I_q) d\hat{R}_q. \tag{6.2}$$

$\hat{R}_q$ is an estimate to the "true" relevance model R_{I_q}; $\pi(D_q, \hat{R}_q)$ is the re-ranking of D_q based on the relevance model estimate; $Pr(\hat{R}_q|I_q)$ is the probability that $\hat{R}_q$ is equal to R_{I_q}.

Equation 6.2 can be instantiated in numerous ways to yield a specific query-performance predictor. We have to (i) derive estimates for the true relevance model ($\hat{R}_q$), (ii) estimate the extent to which these estimates represent the hidden information need ($Pr(\hat{R}_q|I_q)$), and (iii) select measures of similarity between ranked lists. Given a sample of relevance model estimates, we can then approximate Equation 6.2 as follows:

$$U(D_q|I_q) \approx \sum_{\hat{R}_q} Sim\left(\pi(D_q, \hat{R}_q), D_q\right) Pr(\hat{R}_q|I_q). \tag{6.3}$$

Figure 6.1 illustrates the prediction process in the *UEF* framework. Given a query q and the corresponding list of retrieved results D_q, a sample of relevance models are induced from the list. Each relevance model is then used to re-rank D_q, and its quality is estimated as a *representative* of the "true" information need. The similarity of the re-rankings to the original ranking is then measured and scaled by the quality estimation of the relevance model. The (weighted) average of these similarity values provides the final performance prediction.

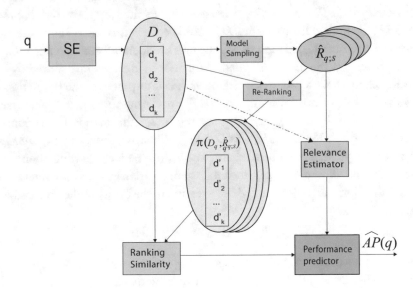

Figure 6.1: A flow diagram of the prediction process in the *UEF* framework.

6.3.2   EVALUATING THE *UEF* FRAMEWORK

In this section, we describe the instantiation applied in (49) to evaluate the *UEF* framework for performance prediction.

6.3.2.1 Relevance model estimation

In general, sampling estimates for the relevance model is done as follows: an estimate is constructed by sampling a set of documents S from D_q. Then, the relevance model estimate constructed from S is the language model induced from S (36), $\hat{R}_{q;S} = Pr(\cdot|S)$, which is a probability distribution over the vocabulary.

In the experiments described below, the sampling strategy from D_q, to define a sampled relevance-model estimate, is based on using all D_q as a single sampled set. The resultant predictor instantiated from Equation 6.3 could be regarded as the *posterior-mode estimate* for the integral in Equation 6.2 (35). In this case, the summation in Equation 6.3 is reduced to one relevance-model estimate only. Hence, the utility prediction is based on measuring the similarity between the original ranking D_q and the re-ranking induced over D_q by the single relevance model estimate (constructed from D_q). This similarity is multiplied by the "quality" of the relevance model estimate, $Pr(\hat{R}_{q;D_q}|I_q)$, i.e., the extent to which this estimate represents the information need.

6.3.2.2 Quality of the relevance model estimate

Estimating the extent to which a relevance-model estimate, $\hat{R}_{q;D_q}$, represents I_q is addressed by adapting four performance predictors, originally proposed for predicting the quality of a result list. These predictors represent the different post-retrieval query-performance prediction paradigms, surveyed in Chapter 5; namely, the *Clarity* method, the *WIG* and *NQC* measures that rely on score distribution, and the query-feedback predictor (*QF*) that is based on ranking robustness.

Clarity measures the quality of $\hat{R}_{q;D_q}$ directly; thus it is the most natural estimator for the relevance model quality. *WIG* and *NQC* both predict the average precision of D_q. Using these predictors for quality estimation is based on the assumption that the higher the AP of D_q, the better $\hat{R}_{q;D_q}$ in representing the true information need.

QF measures the (overlap based) similarity between D_q and a new result list constructed using $\hat{R}_{q;D_q}$ as a query run against the entire corpus. The idea is that a relevance model constructed from a high quality list would not yield a ranking that drifts much from the original ranking. Thus, *QF* can be utilized as a measure for relevance model quality – the less drift the ranking it induces manifests, the more likely it is to represent the information need.

6.3.2.3 Similarity between ranked lists

The remaining task for instantiating Equation 6.2 is the estimation of the similarity $Sim(\pi(D_q, \hat{R}_{q;D_q}), D_q)$ between two rankings of the given result list D_q. Naturally, in the experiments described below, Pearson correlation is used for that task.

6.3.3   RESULTS

The prediction quality of the *UEF*-based predictors, when using the four quality measures for the relevance model estimate, is presented in Table 6.2. Evidently, the *UEF*-based predictors consistently and substantially improve over using the quality measures as predictors in their own right; i.e., to directly predict the search effectiveness of the original list.

For example, using *UEF* with *Clarity* improves prediction quality by more than 30% on average, over the five TREC benchmarks, with respect to direct usage of *Clarity* for performance prediction. Furthermore, the improvements over all four quality measures for the WT10G benchmark is quite striking as it is known to posit a difficult challenge for performance prediction (71); the relative improvements for GOV2, on the other hand, are in general smaller than those for the other collections.

Table 6.2: Prediction quality of *UEF* when fixing the inter-ranking similarity measure to Pearson, and using four predictors for quality estimates. The prediction quality of each predictor, when used to directly predict search effectiveness, is presented for reference in the first row of a block. The best result in a column is boldfaced. From Shtok et al (49).

Predictor	TREC4	TREC5	WT10G	ROBUST	GOV2	avg. improv.
Clarity	0.453	0.42	0.348	0.512	0.433	
UEF(*Clarity*)	0.623	**0.629**	0.483	0.635	0.462	
	(+37.5%)	(+49.8%)	(+38.8%)	(+24%)	(+6.7%)	(+31.4%)
WIG	0.544	0.297	0.376	0.543	0.479	
UEF(*WIG*)	0.638	0.555	0.453	**0.644**	0.458	
	(+17.3%)	(+86.9%)	(+20.5%)	(+18.6%)	(−4.4%)	(+27.8%)
NQC	0.588	0.354	0.488	0.566	0.36	
UEF(*NQC*)	0.641	0.545	0.522	0.619	0.393	
	(+9%)	(+53.9%)	(+6.9%)	(+9.4%)	(+9.2%)	(+17.7%)
QF	0.627	0.414	0.426	0.285	0.476	
UEF(*QF*)	**0.666**	0.538	**0.526**	0.459	**0.491**	
	(+6.2%)	(+29.9%)	(+23.5%)	(+61%)	(+3.1%)	(+24.7%)

6.3.4   COMBINING PREDICTORS IN THE *UEF* MODEL

Integrating *WIG* and *QF* was shown to be of merit (71). As such, an integration yields a predictor for the quality of the initial list from which we construct a relevance model; we can use it in the *UEF* framework as a quality measure. Shtok et al. (49) conducted such an experiment. The resultant predictor is denoted *UEF*(*WIG* +*QF*), where *WIG* +*QF* is the interpolation-based predictor. For comparison, the prediction performance of *UEF*(*WIG*)+ *UEF*(*QF*) that interpolates *UEF*(*WIG*) and *UEF*(*QF*) is also given. Linear interpolation with equal weights is performed in all cases upon the min-max normalized values assigned by predictors. The prediction performance quality values are presented in Table 6.3.

In accordance with previous findings (71), we see in Table 6.3 that integrating *WIG* and *QF* results in prediction performance superior to that of each over most corpora. Using the integrated predictor in the *UEF* framework (*UEF*(*WIG* +*QF*)) yields further prediction improvements for three out of the five corpora. Furthermore, for all corpora, except for GOV2, it is clearly better to integrate *UEF* based predictors — i.e., *UEF(WIG)*) and *UEF(QF)* – than to integrate *WIG* and *QF* directly.

Table 6.3: Integrating predictors using linear interpolation (+). The best result in a column is boldfaced. From (49).

	TREC4	TREC5	WT10G	ROBUST	GOV2
WIG	0.544	0.297	0.376	0.543	0.479
QF	0.627	0.414	0.426	0.285	0.476
WIG +QF	0.676	0.446	0.472	0.503	**0.555**
UEF(WIG +QF)	0.663	0.562	0.513	0.586	0.501
UEF(WIG)+UEF(QF)	**0.679**	**0.591**	**0.521**	**0.591**	0.490

6.4 SUMMARY

This chapter discussed the high potential in combining performance predictors, especially when the different predictors are independent and measure different aspects of the query and the search results. Linear regression has been proposed as a general framework for incorporating predictors. The *UEF* framework, which is based on statistical decision theory, provides an alternative framework for integrating post-retrieval predictors while used as relevance model estimates. The estimate of the relevance model scales the similarity between the re-ranking it induces with the original ranking to provide a performance prediction.

Empirical evaluation shows that combined post-retrieval predictors from both frameworks consistently and substantially improve over using the predictors in their own right. Moreover, the prediction quality of the UEF based predictors are significantly and consistently better than the prediction quality of pre-retrieval and post retrieval predictors presented so far.

CHAPTER 7

A General Model for Query Difficulty

7.1 GEOMETRICAL ILLUSTRATION

An interesting illustration for typical difficulties in retrieval is proposed in (55). We can represent all documents in the collection, including the query, as vectors (points) in the high dimensional vector space. The retrieval process can then be described as finding the k-nearest neighbors of the query, where each neighboring document is scored by inverse proportion to its distance from the query. When relevance information is also given, the retrieval effectiveness can be measured by the fraction of relevant documents from the set of k neighbors. When no such information is available, query performance prediction methods can be applied—based on the geometric pattern of the retrieved set—to predict the expected retrieval effectiveness.

Figure 7.1 illustrates four typical retrieval scenarios in a two-dimensional vector space. The query is marked by a solid square in the middle of the figure; relevant documents are marked by plusses ('+') and non-relevant document by dots ('.'). The points within the circle around the query are the k nearest neighbors retrieved.

In an ideal scenario, the set of relevant documents will be centralized around the query, separated from the rest of the collection. In such a case, the query is "easy" as most nearest neighbors are relevant, and the most relevant documents are similar to the query as well as to each other. Figure 7.1 (a) illustrates this case. Note that all post-retrieval prediction methods are expected to predict high performance for the query in this case as the retrieval set is coherent and separated from the whole collection.

Unfortunately, in real scenarios, it is more likely that only a few of the similar documents to the query are relevant and most are not. Figure 7.1 (b) shows a typical scenario when the nearest neighbors contain relevant and non-relevant documents. Still, the retrieved set is separable from the whole collection; thus we can assume reasonable retrieval (high *Clarity* score).

Figures 7.1 (c) and (d) represent undesirable retrieval scenarios. The first one (c) is the case when the nearest results are too far from the query. Increasing the radius around the query (for accumulating k neighbors) may lead to poor results. Apparently, poor performance can be predicted as the retrieval set is very sensitive to any perturbation in the query or documents, and additionally, score distribution analysis might predict poor performance as the scores of top results are low. The second scenario, (d), is the case when the result set exhibits no unique structure that distinguishes it from the rest of the collection. The lack of cohesiveness is an indication of the low quality of the

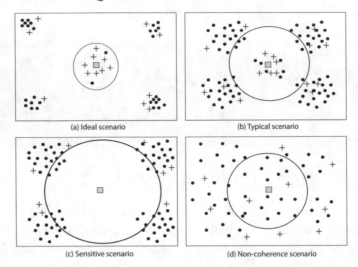

Figure 7.1: Four typical retrieval scenarios. The query is marked by a solid square in the middle of the figure; relevant documents are marked by plusses ('+') and non-relevant document by dots ('.'). The points within the circle around the query are the k nearest neighbors retrieved. Based on (55).

result set. Moreover, we can see that the (d) collection is more difficult than the other collections, as most retrievals from this collection are expected to be poor.

7.2   GENERAL MODEL

A typical information retrieval scenario comprises a collection of documents and a search engine that retrieves documents in response to user queries. Users submitting a query to the search engine have an idea of the information they are trying to find. They are also able to judge the search results according to their relevance to this information need. Thus, the query and the relevant documents are two facets of the same information need.

An alternative general model for query difficulty is suggested by Carmel et al. (12). In this model, the primal object of the model is a *Topic*. A topic is the information pertinent to a defined subject. The topic comprises two objects: a set of queries, Q, and a set of relevant documents, R. The queries are possible expressions reflecting the information need, while the relevant documents contain the information satisfying that need. The topic is also dependent on the specific document collection, C, from which R is chosen. Thus, a topic is denoted as:

$$Topic = (Q, R|C) \tag{7.1}$$

For each topic, it is important to measure how broad the topic is and how well it is separated from the collection. In terms of clustering, this is akin to measuring the in-cluster variability and

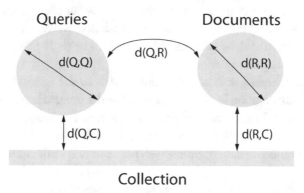

Figure 7.2: A general model of a topic based on the queries, expressing the specific information need, the relevant documents for those queries, the entire collection, and the distances between the sets involved. From (12).

the between-class variability. These measurements can be performed on both facets of the model. An additional measurement, which is of even greater interest, is the distance between the two facets of the model; i.e., the distance between Q and R. We hypothesize that a large distance translates to a difficult topic while a small distance results in an easy topic.

Figure 7.2 shows a schema of the topic difficulty model and the different distances among its elements:

1. $d(Q, C)$ - The distance between the queries, Q, and the collection, C. This distance is analogous to the *simplified Clarity score* (SCS) (25).

2. $d(Q, Q)$ - The distance among the queries, i.e., the diameter of the set Q.

3. $d(R, C)$ - The distance between the relevant documents, R, and the collection, C. This is analogous to the *Clarity* score of the query (14).

4. $d(R, R)$ - The distance among the relevant documents, i.e., the diameter of the set R. This is analogous to the cohesion score (56).

5. $d(Q, R)$ - The distance between the queries, Q, and the relevant documents, R.

The measures $d(Q, C)$, $d(R, C)$, and $d(Q, R)$, as defined above, can be estimated using the KL (or JSD) distance between the language models of the sets Q, R, and C, respectively. Estimating $d(Q, Q)$ and $d(R, R)$ can be done by measuring the set cohesion according to its clustering patterns (56). Section 7.4 discusses an alternative estimation of $d(R, R)$, which is based on the number of clusters in R, for the experiments described below.

In some cases, it is possible to obtain only one of the model objects (Q or R). For example, a search engine manager inspecting the search engine query log has access to the queries regarding a certain topic, but the relevant documents to this topic are not supplied. That is, he has access to the documents in the collection, but the documents are not labeled as relevant to a specific topic. In this case, the model is still very useful, as it is possible to approximate R from the top results retrieved by the search engine for the given queries.

Similarly, a content manager might not have access to the specific queries users are typing while trying to find the information in her site, only to the documents he manages. In such cases, the model can still be used to estimate how easily the information can be found, by estimating $d(R, C)$ and $d(R, R)$ distances. This is similar to the notion of *Findability* in the context of search engine optimization where the objective is to optimize web pages so that their content is optimally findable.

7.3   VALIDATING THE GENERAL MODEL

The general model for query difficulty has been validated by measuring the correlation between the model-induced measurements (JSD distances of the model components) and the median average precision (AP) of all systems that participated in the TREC Terabyte tracks (12). In these tracks, participants searched the GOV2 document collection, experimenting with short queries based on the topic titles while using the TREC topics 701-800 of the 2004 and 2005 Terabyte tracks.

As shown in Figure 7.2, there are five distances of interest in the model. However, because TREC topics provide a single query for each topic, the inter-query distance could not be used. Thus, four distances and their correlations with AP were evaluated.

Table 7.1 shows the Pearson and the *Spearman's-ρ* correlation values for each of the distances with the median AP. All correlations with an absolute value larger than 0.164 are statistically significant at $p < 0.05$. *Clarity*, the distance of the relevant documents from the collection is by far the most important factor influencing topic average precision. The explanation for this phenomena is that a longer distance reflects better separability of the set of relevant documents from the entire collection. The distance of the query to the collection, $d(Q, C)$, and the number of topic aspects, $d(R, R)$, have a lower, yet substantial, effect on precision, while the distance of the query to the relevant documents, $d(Q, R)$ has almost no effect.

Table 7.1: The correlation between the model distances and the median AP of all TREC participants in the 2004 and 2005 Terabyte tracks. From (12).

Distance	TREC median AP	
	Pearson	*Spearman's-ρ*
$d(Q, C)$	0.298	0.292
$d(R, C)$	0.331	0.323
$d(Q, R)$	-0.019	0.004
$d(R, R)$	0.119	0.155
Combined	0.476	

We note that the signs of the regression coefficient show that a longer distance between the queries and the relevant documents from the collection results in a higher AP, while a shorter distance between queries and documents results in lower AP. Interestingly, a larger number of aspects correlates positively with AP.

The values of Pearson's non-parametric correlation and *Spearman's-ρ* parametric correlation are remarkably similar, suggesting that the values are linearly correlated. The Pearson correlation of AP with the combination of the four model parameters (the row denoted by "Combined") is relatively high, suggesting that the model captures important aspects of the query difficulty.

7.4 THE RELATIONSHIP BETWEEN ASPECT COVERAGE AND QUERY DIFFICULTY

Most retrieval models assume that the relevance of a document is independent of the relevance of other documents. In reality, however, this assumption rarely holds; relevant documents can relate to different aspects of the topic; hence, the entire utility of the result set strongly depends on the number of relevant aspects it covers.

The *aspect coverage* problem has to do with finding documents that cover as many different aspects of the topic as possible. This problem has been investigated in the interactive track of TREC-7 where the purpose was to study how systems can best cover all relevant aspects of a topic (41). Zhai et al. (66) describe some evaluation measures for aspect coverage of a given result set.

The *aspect coverage* problem is another facet of query difficulty. This is clearly demonstrated by the failure categories identified in the RIA workshop (20), given in Table 1.1, where five of the nine failure categories relate to poor aspect coverage. Therefore, the difficulty of a topic can be measured by the number of different aspects related to the topic.

According to the general model of query difficulty, the broadness of the relevant results is measured by the distance $d(R, R)$. A small distance would reflect a coherent set of relevant documents, all providing the same information. However, this measure suffers from the drawback that identical (or extremely similar) documents are very close together, despite adding no information to the user.

Thus, aspect coverage can be used as an alternative indication of $d(R, R)$. Given a topic with the set of relevant documents, the number of topic aspects is estimated by clustering the relevant documents. Using the square root of the JSD as a distance measure between documents, the set of documents is clustered and the broadness of the topic is estimated by the number of clusters formed. This is, of course, only an approximation since it assumes that every document focuses on one aspect only. However, in reality, a document could describe more than one aspect of a topic.

In the experiments described below, we use the number of aspects (the number of clusters) of the topic's relevant documents to estimate the diameter $d(R, R)$ of the difficulty model.

7.5   VALIDATING THE RELATIONSHIP BETWEEN ASPECT COVERAGE AND QUERY DIFFICULTY

To estimate the relationship between the query difficulty model distances and topic aspect coverage, the correlation between the model distances and the number of aspects covered by the top results retrieved by the search engine was measured for the 100 GOV2 topics.

Given a ranked list of results for a query retrieved by the retrieval system, the number of covered aspects is measured as follows:

1. Find all aspects of the topic by clustering R, the set of its relevant documents, assuming each cluster relates to a different aspect.

2. For each aspect, mark the top result in the ranking belonging to the corresponding cluster as relevant, and mark all other relevant documents in the result set belonging to that cluster as non-relevant. In this way, every aspect covered by the result set has one representative in the ranking.

3. Compute average precision using the new marked documents. The aspect coverage measure promotes rankings that cover more aspects and also takes into consideration the ranks of the relevant documents. A ranking that includes documents from many different aspects on top of the list is preferred over a ranking containing documents that redundantly cover the same aspect.

Table 7.2 shows the correlation between the difficulty model distances and the aspect coverage of top results for the 100 GOV2 topics.

Table 7.2: The correlation between the model distances and the aspect coverage of top results for the 100 GOV2 topics. From (12).

Distance	Aspect Coverage	
	Pearson	Spearman's-ρ
$d(Q, C)$	0.047	0.047
$d(R, C)$	0.143	0.194
$d(Q, R)$	-0.271	-0.285
$d(R, R)$	-0.364	-0.418
Combined	0.482	

As Table 7.2 shows, the distance between the query and the relevant documents, $d(Q, R)$, and the broadness of the topic, $d(R, R)$, have the most significant influence on the ability to retrieve many topic aspects. (All correlations with an absolute value larger than 0.164 are statistically significant at $p < 0.05$.) As expected, the more aspects a topic has (larger $d(R, R)$), the harder it is to retrieve all of them. The separation of the query and the relevant documents from the collection ($d(Q, C)$

and $d(R, C)$, respectively) has a very minor role in aspect coverage. Interestingly, the combined correlation of all four measurements is extremely similar to that of regular AP and is a relatively high value.

7.6   SUMMARY

This chapter addressed a general model that captures the main components of a query and the relations between those components and query difficulty. The three components of a topic are the textual expression describing the information need (the query or queries), the set of relevant documents of the topic, and the entire collection of documents. We showed that query difficulty depends on the distances between those components. The larger the distance of the queries and the relevant documents from the entire collection, the better the topic can be answered. The smaller the distance between the queries and relevant documents, and the smaller the number of different aspects in the relevant documents (a smaller $d(R, R)$), more topic aspects can be anticipated to be covered.

The difficulty model described in this chapter is based on the relationship between the main topic components. However, there are many more important features affecting topic difficulty that the current model ignores. For example, ambiguity of the query terms. Extending the model to encapsulate other facets of topic difficulty is still an open challenge.

CHAPTER 8

Applications of Query Difficulty Estimation

So far, we have addressed query difficulty estimation as a goal in its own right, i.e., the ability to predict query performance using various estimators. In this chapter, we show how such information can be used for various applications that improve and enhance retrieval.

8.1   FEEDBACK: TO THE USER AND TO THE SYSTEM

The most straightforward application of query difficulty estimation is as direct feedback to the user. The idea is to present a user with immediate feedback on the predicted performance of a query, so that he can decide to reformulate the query or to use another source of information when results are expected to be poor. In addition to the top results presented to the user, the search engine can also provide (visual) feedback on the predicted query performance. In this way, users are informed about poor retrieval and can act accordingly. An example of such feedback is presented in Figure 8.1.

Additionally, performance prediction technologies can be used by search engines to improve their interaction with their users. For example, query refinement is an interactive process that can be used to narrow down the scope of search results, by expansion or modification. Terms for refinement can be extracted from various sources such as query logs, collocates of the query terms, external resources, and more. Given a query and a set of candidate terms for refinement, the expected utility of each term can be estimated based on predicting the performance of the query refined with that term. Some preliminary work has been conducted in this direction (31).

Similarly, personalizing the search results should be better performed selectively based on the query and the specific user. There is a lot of variation across queries in the benefits that the user can gain through personalization. For some queries, everyone who issues the query is looking for the same thing. For other queries, different people look for different results even though they express their need in the same way. Teevan et al. (52) studied a variety of features of the query, the results, and the user's interaction history, as inferred from the system's query log. These features were used to build a predictive model to identify queries that can benefit from personalization.

Feedback based applications that are based on query difficulty estimation have not, to the best of our knowledge, been put to commercial use yet. However, we believe that this is only a matter of time before this technology emerges. It will be interesting to see how such feedback can be utilized by real users to improve their general search experience.

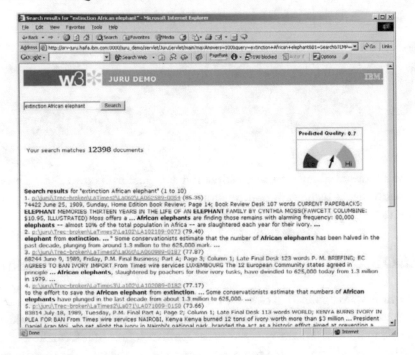

Figure 8.1: Snapshot of a search results screen with estimation of the query difficulty, provided as feedback to the user.

8.2   FEDERATION AND METASEARCH

Another application of query difficulty estimation is *metasearch* and *federation*. Instead of retrieving information from a single information source using one search engine, one can utilize multiple search engines or a single search engine retrieving documents from a plethora of document collections. A scenario where multiple engines are used is known as metasearch, while the scenario where a single engine retrieves from multiple collections is known as federation. In both these scenarios, the final result of the retrieval effort needs to be a single, unified ranking of documents, based on several ranked lists.

Metasearch is of major interest when retrieving information from the Web. For example, it is desirable to have a single interface for submitting a query to many Web search engines such as Yahoo! Google, and Bing, and receiving a unified list of results based on the combined results returned by these engines. The unified list should include the most relevant documents from each of the lists returned by the individual search engines. Dreilinger & Howe (17) give an overview of metasearch engines on the Web.

Federation of document collections is addressed mainly in the context of retrieving information from a multitude of specialized datasets, using a single search engine. Several datasets may hold information which cannot be unified due to scalability, privacy, or security issues. It is therefore required that a single search engine retrieves documents from each of these datasets for a given query, and merges them into a unified list.

One approach to using query difficulty estimation in federation and metasearch is to apply a query performance predictor for each dataset and search engine combination. When a query is executed, the ranked list of documents is returned from each dataset and search engine combination and the prediction of query difficulty is computed for each. The predicted performance is used for weighting the retrieved list of documents and the final ranking is built by merging the lists using these weights. This allows for a query-by-query weight for each search engine and document collection pair. Yom-Tov et al. (65) applied this strategy for both scenarios, using a predictor based on average document frequency of the query terms ($avgIDF$) and the overlap between the result list returned for a full query and that returned for individual query terms (however, since this method is independent of the prediction method, other prediction methods could equally have been applied). In that paper, this fusion approach was shown to improve metasearch (as measured by P@10) by 7% over the best single search engine and by 12% over other metasearch strategies. The corresponding improvement in federation was 15%. Interestingly, a noticeable improvement in performance was found using federation with query difficulty estimation over the performance obtained from a single index representing the unified document collection. This suggests that the federation with fusion strategy, based on performance prediction, is superior to a one-index search solution for heterogeneous document collections, even when the collections can be integrated together.

One alternative to metasearch is to select the best search engine for a given query. This is the approach taken by White et al. (62), who built a predictor for choosing one of several web search engines for a given query. In their work, queries were represented by numerous features that describe attributes of the query, the search engine, the results returned by each search engine, and features that capture the similarity between the query and results. Using a linear classifier to learn a predictor that categorizes each query for the most appropriate search engine, significant improvement in accuracy was obtained, over the accuracy of results while using a single engine for all queries. In fact, according to the results of this work, half of all queries could be improved by selecting the correct search engine; although, in practice, since the classifier is not always correct, a much smaller improvement in accuracy is expected.

In a similar vein, Berger and Savoy (5) used different translation tools to translate queries from English to Spanish and German, in order to retrieve documents in these languages. They showed that there is a wide variability in performance of the different translation tools, both on average and for each query specifically. This suggests using query difficulty estimation to identify which of the tools is most likely to be correct for each query. Using features based on term frequency in the target collection and on linguistic analysis (existence of personal or geographic proper nouns in the translation, presence of proper names, etc.), a logistic-regression predictor was built and applied. The result showed an impressive improvement in performance over the best single translation tool.

8.3   CONTENT ENHANCEMENT USING MISSING CONTENT ANALYSIS

A fundamental question we addressed in Chapter 1 is why a query is difficult for a search engine. Briefly, this is due to ambiguity, poor relationships between query and content, and insufficient content. In this section, we address an application of query difficulty estimation to identifying the queries with insufficient content.

There are some queries for which all the results returned by the search engine are irrelevant, simply because no relevant content exists in the document collection. For example, a collection of medical documents has few, if any, relevant documents for queries in the domain of computer hardware support. In such cases, it is important to either notify the user that no relevant content exists or to automatically augment the document collection with relevant information from an external source such as the Web.

One approach to identifying missing content was suggested by Yom-Tov et al. (64). In that paper, a binary approach to missing content was taken; that is, either there were relevant documents for queries, or there were none. In practice, this approach was validated by removing the relevant documents for some queries, while keeping the relevant documents of other queries. A query difficulty predictor was then trained to identify the patterns associated with missing content and applied to new queries. The performance of the predictor showed that missing content can indeed be identified by training an appropriate query difficulty estimator.

Another approach to finding queries with missing content was taken by Spangler and Kreulen (51), who analyzed a help-desk knowledge base by scoring queries according to their nearest document in the collection of existing solutions. Queries with no close solutions were considered to be lacking in corpus-pertinent content.

Beyond reporting queries suspected of missing content, a logical step, especially in the setting of a specialized or inter-organizational document collection, is to augment the collection with relevant documents from a third source such as the Web. If done correctly, over time, these supplements to the collection will improve responsiveness to users, without compromising the collection's focus.

Since user needs change dynamically over time and new missing content queries are expected to appear on a regular basis, the collection repository should be updated regularly to satisfy those new needs. There is a definite need for a tool that can identify new popular information needs not covered well by the current content. Such a tool would dynamically analyze the query log of the system, identify missing content queries, and then direct the system to enrich its data, thereby improving its ability to better satisfy its users' needs.

The quality of the content can also be evaluated in relation to a given taxonomy of knowledge. A taxonomy may refer to either a hierarchical classification of topics or the principles underlying the classification of the content into those specific topics. Given a taxonomy that specifies desired knowledge, the repository can be analyzed by identifying the topics in the taxonomy that are not well covered by the current content. Important topics that are not well covered by the existing content can be used to direct the system to enrich the repository to better cover those missing topics.

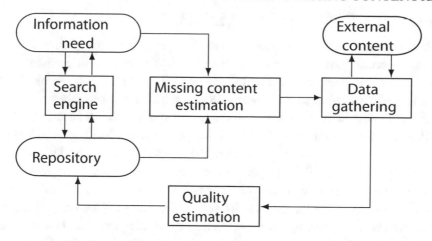

Figure 8.2: Outline of a system for information augmentation

As an example, consider a portal intended for use by system administrators (SAs). The portal lets SAs search for technical information that can help them solve daily problems occurring on the servers for which they are responsible. The information is obtained from multiple sources such as internal problem ticketing systems, server monitoring records, and other technical documents. In such a narrow domain, the usability of the portal depends on its ability to support the information needs of the SAs and provide the right information at the right time so SAs can solve problems within a reasonable time. Therefore, identifying and eliminating knowledge gaps between the information existing in the portal and that required by the SAs is a crucial factor in providing fast and reliable support to customers. On the other hand, a general purpose document collection will not serve its audience well. Therefore, it is important that all relevant information, and only the relevant information, be brought to the portal.

Such an information augmentation system, developed by Carmel et al. (13) is shown in Figure 8.2. The first component of the system identifies topic areas that are missing content. Once missing content topics are identified, they are sent to the data gathering component so a search can be conducted for relevant content. The data gathering component uses an external information source to find relevant content. This content is passed to the local repository via a quality estimation component, which assesses whether the content found by the data gathering component is indeed relevant to the topics lacking in content. The appropriate content can then be added to the local repository.

The precision of the search engine used in (13) improved four-fold over time, by identifying missing content and augmenting it with pages from the Web. This shows the immense value that can be gained by building domain specific repositories, which are updated with relevant information from general repositories.

8.4   SELECTIVE QUERY EXPANSION

Automatic query expansion is a widely used method for improving the quality of search and has been shown to improve (average) retrieval performance. A popular post-retrieval expansion approach, termed *pseudo-relevance feedback* (PRF) (39), considers the (few) top-ranked documents to be relevant, and uses them to expand the query. In general, PRF has been shown to improve query performance; however, it has not been used in many operational systems because of the fact that it can greatly degrade the performance of a system for certain individual queries. For many queries, PRF deteriorates query results due to *query drift* (39), which relates to the changes in the focus of the query in its expanded form. This happens either because non-relevant documents infiltrate into the top results or relevant results contain irrelevant aspects of the query's original intention.

Many PRF methods employ the *Rocchio formula* for query expansion (46). In Rocchio, the query and documents are represented as vectors in the same vector-space, and the expanded query is obtained by combining the original query and the centroid of the top results. This adds new terms to the query and reweighs the original terms. Increasing the relative weight of the original query compared to the centroid's weight in the Rocchio formula "anchors" the expanded query to the original query, thus discouraging the query drift.

Formally, given a query q, and the top-k results D_q^k, a new query is formulated as follows:

$$q' = (1 - \alpha)\, q + \alpha \left(\frac{1}{k} \sum_{d \in D_q^k} d \right) \tag{8.1}$$

where α is known as the feedback coefficient that balances the original query with the centroid of the top results.

PRF methods work well when the highest ranked documents are relevant to the query, and thus the frequent terms in them may correctly expand the user's original query as to better reflect its scope. Unfortunately, for poor performing queries, the highest ranked documents will be irrelevant, and thus it may lead to query drift.

Hence, it is not beneficial to apply PRF for every query. Instead, it is expected that selectively applying it to those queries that are predicted to be "easy" while not applying them to other queries will produce better results than either applying PRF to all queries or not applying it at all.

This is the approach taken in several studies. Amati el al. (1) set a threshold on the predicted difficulty, beyond which queries would be expanded. In this approach, only "easy" queries, i.e., those with highly predicted performance, are expanded. In contrast, a classifier was trained in (64) to identify queries for which PRF might be beneficial, based on a training set where queries were assessed as to the increase or decrease in performance caused by expansion. He and Ounis (26) developed a method that combines metasearch with selective query expansion. In their work, two collections were used for retrieval: a local, preferred collection and an external collection. A decision mechanism was used to decide on one of three strategies: retrieve from the local collection, perform query expansion using the local collection, or perform query expansion using the external collection.

The decision on which of the options should be chosen was based on the *avgICTF* statistics of the query: If this was low for both collections, no expansion was used, and retrieval was based on the local collection. If it was high, the collection with higher *avgICTF* value was chosen for retrieval, and expansion was performed. This approach was shown to work with some collections, but it brought no gain with others. In all these cases, the gain obtained over the baselines (not applying expansion at all or applying it to all queries) was marginal, indicating that although selective query expansion has value, additional investigation is required to obtain more robust methods.

8.4.1   SELECTIVE EXPANSION BASED ON QUERY DRIFT ESTIMATION

A different method for predicting the success of PRF for individual queries was taken by Cronen-Townsend et al. (15). This method requires a system to run both the unexpanded and expanded queries, and then compares the two retrieved lists to decide which results to present to the user. Instead of directly predicting the success of an expanded query, this approach measures how far the language model of the expanded query's results strayed from the language model of the unexpanded query's results. The rational, which is in line with the *query feedback* predictor (71) described in Chapter 5, is that if an expanded query's model is very far from the unexpanded query's model; this may be an indication for query drift.

The comparison between the language models is based on the distribution of the important terms used for expansion, which are those with the largest influence on the *Clarity* score of the query. When the important terms are less frequent in the expanded model than in the unexpanded model, we can hypothesize that the expanded retrieval is less likely to reflect the original meaning of the query. In this case, the original results are presented to the user. In contrast, when the frequency of the important terms has grown, the expanded retrieval is thus more likely to be useful; therefore, the expanded results are given. In practice, this method shows only marginal improvements over expanding all queries. This means that the idea of "strayed" query results is useful to some extent in identifying cases where expanded queries failed, they are not the only factor in determining the success or failure of expansion.

Measuring the query drift of the expanded query, based on its language model, can be taken further. A large set of relevance models for each query can be generated by varying the parameters' values of some expansion method, and then selecting the one that is predicted to perform the best for expansion. Winaver et al. (63) show that this multi-model selection strategy yields performance that is almost indistinguishable from that of a manually optimized relevance model.

8.4.2   ADAPTIVE USE OF PSEUDO RELEVANCE FEEDBACK

The attempts described above for selective query expansion focus on deciding for each query whether to expand it or not. This is a binary decision that is based on the predicted performance of the expanded query. An alternative adaptive approach, suggested by Lv and Zhai (37), selectively decides how much to expand a given query, by dynamically predicting the optimal α, the feedback coefficient.

Specifically, this method estimates a potentially different feedback coefficient for each query and each set of expanded documents, rather than manually setting it to a fixed constant.

The value of the feedback coefficient was estimated for every query, using three types of query difficulty features as input to the prediction module:

1. Discrimination of the query: the more discriminative the query, the more tolerant it is to adding information from relevant documents.

2. Discrimination of feedback documents: clearer feedback documents are likely to be more useful for adding to the query.

3. Divergence between query and feedback documents: dissimilarity between the query and documents indicates that the query was too narrow, and that a larger feedback coefficient is required.

Lv and Zhai generated a set of features from the above-mentioned categories, and trained a logistic regression algorithm, which finds the best weights for combining the features to predict the correct feedback coefficient for a given query. By following this direct route to predicting the correct feedback coefficient, they were able to achieve a significant improvement in retrieval compared to cases where the feedback coefficient was set to a fixed value. They concluded that the three categories are all very important as each captures another aspect of the query and the top results, and the proposed adaptive relevance feedback is more robust and effective than the regular fixed-coefficient feedback.

8.5   OTHER USES OF QUERY DIFFICULTY PREDICTION

The ability to predict the difficulty of a query, even if the accuracy of the prediction is not extremely high, opens the door to several novel applications. We describe some here.

Collaborative filtering is the ability to recommend new content to users, based on the preferences of a larger population. For example, movies may be recommended to a person, based on the movies people similar to him found interesting. A core problem in this field is determining what constitutes a similarity between people. Such similarity may be based on demographic information or the degree to which users liked or disliked similar items.

Bellogin and Castells (3) used a modification of the *Clarity* score (14) to measure the lack of ambiguity in a users' preference. In an analogy to query difficulty, an "easy" user is one whose preferences are clear-cut, and thus contributes much to a neighbor. As an illustration, a user who is only interested in action movies can give a clearer recommendation on these types of movies than a user with broader interests. The *Clarity* of a user is then used to weight his recommendation to other users. An evaluation performed by the authors showed that this method improves the recommendations when looking at a small set of nearest neighbors, but it does not make a difference when averaged over the whole population. This might be the effect of averaging over many people, which cancels some of the noise associated with ambiguous users.

Queries submitted to commercial search engines usually contain one to three terms. Longer queries may be more focused, but in other cases, they contain terms which degrade retrieval performance by adding irrelevant terms to the query. Kumaran and Carvalho (33) attempted to identify these irrelevant query terms using performance prediction. Their method was to create 2^N queries from each query with N original terms. Each query was then described by a series of attributes such as the number of sub-query terms, the *Clarity* score (14), mutual information, and the average inverse document frequency of sub-query terms. A predictor was then trained to rank the sub-queries as to their relative retrieval performance using the attributes of each sub-query. The end result is that a given query can be divided into sub-queries, and the most likely query is identified using performance prediction. Kumaran and Carvalho showed an 8% improvement in retrieval performance and, furthermore, that the *Clarity* score was the most influential feature for ranking sub-queries.

8.6   SUMMARY

This chapter discusses several applications developed recently that utilize query performance prediction. While traditional approaches handle all queries equally, these new applications can dynamically choose the right handling approach for each query based on its predicted difficulty. This trend is likely to grow with coming improvements in prediction methods; hence much more selective applications are expected to appear in the near future that are based on query performance prediction.

Prediction based applications have not yet been adopted by commercial vendors for the general public, and they are mostly used by the research community. This is probably due to the brief time this technology has existed and the assumption that it is not sufficiently mature to be productized. However, the advantages of performance prediction methods are so clear that we can safely assume that this technology will find its way to the market very soon.

CHAPTER 9

Summary and Conclusions

9.1 SUMMARY

Query difficulty estimation is a new emerging area of research that has recently attracted a lot of attention in the IR field. While traditionally IR research mainly focuses on evaluating the relevance of each document to a query, independently of the other documents, the new performance prediction approaches attempt to evaluate the quality of the whole result list to the query. Such evaluation is beneficial for many IR tasks, including a feedback to the end user on the expected quality of retrieved results, a feedback to the search system which can assess its performance at retrieval time, before conducting an intensive process such as query expansion, a feedback to system administrators for taking care of problematic cases such as missing content queries, and for IR applications which can serve dynamically and selectively each query based on its predicted performance.

Query performance prediction is an extremely ambitious task as many factors affect the quality of a ranked list of documents in satisfying the user's information need. These include the number of relevant documents in the list, the rank of those relevant documents, and the inner relations between them, especially for informational queries where users seek for results that cover many different aspects of their needs. The numerous factors that affect the query difficulty can be roughly categorized to those that relate to the query (e.g. ambiguity), to the data (e.g., heterogeneity), to the search system (e.g., inappropriate retrieval method), and to the inter-relations between those components.

In this lecture, we surveyed the current state-of-the-art research on query difficulty estimation for IR. We began by discussing the reasons that cause search engines to fail for some of the queries, and we reviewed several reasons for the high variability in performance among queries as well as among systems. We then summarized several approaches for query performance prediction, and we classified prediction methods to pre-retrieval methods and post-retrieval methods. Pre-retrieval approaches predict the quality of the search results before the search takes place, by analyzing the query text and term statistics. Post-retrieval methods, which have the benefit of access to the search results, are usually more expensive in terms of computational need, as results are analyzed after retrieval. However, these methods are directly applied to the actual results, which means that they are more suitable for identifying inconsistency, incoherency, and other characteristics that reflect low performance.

The common methodology for evaluating the prediction quality of a performance predictor is based on measuring the linear and the rank correlation between the actual performance and the predicted performance of a retrieval system, over a given set of testing queries. We reviewed the results of various evaluation studies conducted over several TREC benchmarks. These results show that state-of-the-art existing predictors are able to identify difficult queries, i.e. to predict their poor performance, by demonstrating a reasonable prediction quality as reflected by the correlation with actual performance. However, prediction quality is still moderate and should be substantially improved in order to be widely used in IR tasks.

Current linguistic-based predictors, which evaluate linguistic features of the query terms (e.g., lexical ambiguity) do not exhibit meaningful correlation with query performance (40; 21), as reflected by the low correlation between actual to predicted performance. This is quite surprising as intuitively poor performance can be expected for ambiguous queries. There is still no good theoretical explanation for this failure. Further research on query linguistic analysis for performance prediction is needed.

In contrast, statistical features such as *sumSCQ*, the similarity of the corpus to the query, and *maxVar*, the maximum variance of query term weights over the documents in collection, have relatively significant predictive ability of performance prediction (68). These pre-retrieval predictors, and a few others, exhibit comparable performance to post-retrieval methods such as *Clarity*, *QF*, *WIG*, and *NQC*. This is counter-intuitive as post-retrieval methods are exposed to much more information than pre-retrieval methods. However, an important insight from the evaluation studies cited in this work is that the prediction quality of all predictors is sensitive to the sets of testing queries used for evaluation, to the datasets, and to the specific method used for retrieval. Thus, current state-of-the-art predictors still suffer from low robustness in prediction quality. This robustness, as well as the moderate prediction quality of existing predictors, are two of the greatest challenges in query difficulty prediction, that should be further explored in the future.

The moderate performance of existing predictors led to the question of whether combining several predictors together may improve prediction quality, especially when the different predictors are independent and measure different aspects of the query and the search results. We reviewed two combination approaches. The first is based on linear regression of several predictors where the regression task is to learn how to optimally combine the predicted performance values in order to best fit them to the actual performance values (21). The quality of the combined predictor did not outperform the best single predictors, probably due to the spareness of the training data, which over-represents the lower end of the performance values.

The second combination approach we discussed is the *UEF* framework that is based on statistical decision theory (49). This framework measures the utility to the user which is expected from a given result list by multiplying two factors. The first one is the extent to which the corresponding relevance model represents the hidden information need. The second is the similarity between the original ranking and the re-ranking this relevance model induces over the list. The quality of a given relevance model can be approximated by any post-retrieval predictor, and the similarity between two ranks can be measured by any rank correlation measure. Empirical evaluation shows that predictors instantiated from the *UEF* framework consistently and substantially improve prediction quality over using the quality measures as predictors at their own right.

Finally, we discussed a few applications that utilize query difficulty estimators by handling each query individually based on its estimated difficulty. We gave an overview of several selective methods that dynamically invoke the right retrieval process for each query based on its predicted performance, instead of handling all queries equally. These methods that 1) attempt to find the best terms for query refinement by measuring the expected gain in performance for each candidate term (31), 2) decide whether to expand the query or not based on predicted performance of the expanded query (1; 64; 15; 37), and 3) personalize the query selectively, only in cases that personalization is expected bring value (52). Other types of applications we surveyed are based on collection enhancement guided by the identification of missing content queries in the systems' query log (13), and the fusion of search results from several sources based on their predicted quality (65). We believe that in the future, as prediction quality increases, we will see many more IR applications that employ this new technology for providing better services to their customers.

9.2   WHAT NEXT?

Most research conducted so far on query difficulty estimation has been focused on predicting the performance of informational, TREC style queries over several TREC corpora. Predicting the performance of other types of queries has attracted much less attention, with the exception of the study on performance prediction of *Web-based queries* using visual features of the Web search results such as titles, snippets, etc. (28), and the study on the performance prediction for *navigational queries* (7) over the GOV2 collection (71). Predicting the performance for other query types and other data types, has not attracted much attention of the research community so far. The difficulty of semi-structured queries (e.g., *Xpath*, or *Xquery* queries) is an interesting topic to explore as the notion of relevance in this domain is different than the typical notion of relevance in IR, as is the definition of successful retrieval. Similarly, performance prediction over domain-specific collections (e.g., in the healthcare domain) is a challenge in its own right, as domain-specific knowledge can contribute to the prediction process. Multimedia search over images, audio, and video files, is another interesting domain to explore for performance prediction technology.

Furthermore, all prediction methods described in this paper only consider the query, the result list, and the collection. However, user satisfaction from the search results is affected by many other factors such as geo-spatial features, temporal aspects, personal parameters, and more. We hypothesize the emergence of new performance predictors that take such parameters into account while predicting the utility of search results to a specific user in a specific context.

The underlying search scenario assumed by all current existing performance predictors is the independent lookup paradigm for which the query is treated as a one-time conception of the searcher's information need. However, a real-life search session typically contains multiple query iterations, post-query browsing, and result examination. In new search paradigms that have emerged recently, such as *multifaceted search*, or *exploratory search*, the information-seeking process is considered an iterative process where users interact with the system through a sequence of actions such as search, browse and refinement. The utility of the iterative session depends on the quality of the search results, as provided by the search engine, and on the user responses. Predicting the effectiveness of such an iterative process has not been explored yet, to the best of our knowledge.

9.3 CONCLUDING REMARKS

Research on query difficulty estimation has begun only a few years ago with the pioneering work of Cronen-Townsend et. al on *Clarity* (14). Since then this subfield has attracted a lot of interest, and it has found its place at the center of IR research, as demonstrated by the volume of related work. These studies have revealed alternative prediction approaches, new evaluation methodologies, and novel applications that benefit from performance prediction technology.

In this lecture, we surveyed the main research directions taken in this area and covered existing performance prediction methods, some evaluation studies, existing applications, and some anticipations on future directions in the field. We tried to summarize the state-of-the-art research conducted on query difficulty estimation, exposing the reader to coherent unified picture on its current status. While the progress we see is enormous already, performance prediction is still challenging and far from being solved. Much more accurate predictors are required in order to be widely adopted by IR tasks. For that, we still need a better understanding to what makes a query difficult. There is room for new research directions and ideas. We hope that this lecture will contribute to increase interest in query difficulty estimation.

Bibliography

[1] Giambattista Amati, Claudio Carpineto, and Giovanni Romano. Query difficulty, robustness and selective application of query expansion. In *Proceedings of the European Conference on Information Retrieval (ECIR 2004)*, pages 127–137. Springer, 2004. 28, 60, 67

[2] Javed A. Aslam and Virgiliu Pavlu. Query hardness estimation using Jensen-Shannon divergence among multiple scoring functions. In *Proceedings of the European Conference on Information Retrieval (ECIR 2007)*, pages 198–209, 2007. DOI: 10.1007/978-3-540-71496-5_20 31

[3] Alejandro Bellogin and Pablo Castells. Predicting neighbor goodness in collaborative filtering. In *Flexible Query Answering Systems (FQAS)*, 2009. DOI: 10.1007/978-3-642-04957-6_52 62

[4] Michael Bendersky and W. Bruce Croft. Discovering key concepts in verbose queries. In *Proceedings of the 31st annual international ACM SIGIR conference on Research and development in information retrieval (SIGIR 2008)*, pages 491–498, Singapore, Singapore, 2008. ACM. DOI: 10.1145/1390334.1390419 17

[5] Pierre-Yves Berger and Jacques Savoy. Selecting automatically the best query translations. In *8th International Conference on Computer-Assisted Information Retrieval (Recherche d'Information et ses Applications) (RIAO 2007)*, 2007. 57

[6] Yaniv Bernstein, Bodo Billerbeck, Steven Garcia, Nicholas Lester, Falk Scholer, and Justin Zobel. RMIT university at TREC 2005: Terabyte and robust track. In *Proceedings of 14th Text REtrieval Conference TREC-14*, 2005. 32

[7] Andrei Broder. A taxonomy of web search. *SIGIR Forum*, 36(2):3–10, 2002. DOI: 10.1145/792550.792552 67

[8] Chris Buckley. The TREC-9 Query track. In *Proceedings of 9th Text REtrieval Conference (TREC-9)*, 2000. 27

[9] Chris Buckley. Reliable information access final workshop report. Technical report, Northeast Regional Research Center (NRRC), 2004. 4

[10] Chris Buckley, Gerard Salton, James Allan, and Amit Singhal. Automatic query expansion using SMART: TREC3. In *Proceedings of the 3rd Text REtrieval Conference (TREC-3)*, pages 69–80, 1994. 22

[11] David Carmel, Ian Soboroff, and Elad Yom-Tov. SIGIR workshop report: Workshop on query prediction and its applications. In *Proceedings of the 28th annual international conference on Research and development in information retrieval (SIGIR 2005)*, Salvador, Bahia, Brazil, 2005. 77

[12] David Carmel, Elad Yom-Tov, Adam Darlow, and Dan Pelleg. What makes a query difficult? In *Proceedings of the 29th annual international ACM SIGIR conference on Research and development in information retrieval (SIGIR 2006)*, pages 390–397, Seattle, Washington, USA, 2006. ACM. DOI: 10.1145/1148170.1148238 6, 13, 23, 28, 35, 48, 49, 50, 52, 77

[13] David Carmel, Elad Yom-Tov, and Haggai Roitman. Enhancing digital libraries using missing content analysis. In *Proceedings of the Joint Conference on Digital Libraries (JCDL 2008)*, pages 1–10, Pittsburgh, Pennsylvania, 2008. ACM. DOI: 10.1145/1378889.1378891 59, 67, 77

[14] Steve Cronen-Townsend, Yun Zhou, and W. Bruce Croft. Predicting query performance. In *Proceedings of the 25th annual international ACM SIGIR conference on Research and development in information retrieval (SIGIR 2002)*, pages 299–306, Tampere, Finland, 2002. ACM. DOI: 10.1145/564376.564429 26, 27, 28, 35, 49, 62, 63, 68

[15] Steve Cronen-Townsend, Yun Zhou, and W. Bruce Croft. Precision prediction based on ranked list coherence. *Information Retrieval*, 9(6):723–755, 2006. DOI: 10.1007/s10791-006-9006-4 27, 28, 61, 67

[16] Fernando Diaz. Performance prediction using spatial autocorrelation. In *Proceedings of the 30th annual international ACM SIGIR conference on Research and development in information retrieval (SIGIR 2007)*, pages 583–590, Amsterdam, The Netherlands, 2007. ACM. DOI: 10.1145/1277741.1277841 23, 32, 35, 41

[17] Daniel Dreilinger and Adele Howe. Experiences with selecting search engines using meta-search. *ACM Transactions on Information Systems*, 15(3):195–222, 1997. DOI: 10.1145/256163.256164 56

[18] Christiane Fellbaum. *WordNet: An Electronic Lexical Database*. Bradford Books, 1998. 17

[19] Donna Harman. What we have learned, and not learned, from TREC. BCS-IRSG 22nd Annual Colloquium on Information Retrieval Research, April 2002. 2

[20] Donna Harman and Chris Buckley. Overview of the reliable information access workshop. *Information Retrieval*, 12(6):615–641, 2009. DOI: 10.1007/s10791-009-9101-4 3, 51

[21] Claudia Hauff. *Predicting the Effectiveness of Queries and Retrieval Systems*. PhD thesis, University of Twente, February 2010. xi, 19, 20, 22, 23, 24, 27, 29, 40, 66

[22] Claudia Hauff, Leif Azzopardi, and Djoerd Hiemstra. The combination and evaluation of query performance prediction methods. In *Proceedings of the 31th European Conference on IR Research on Advances in Information Retrieval (ECIR 2009)*, pages 301–312, Toulouse, France, 2009. Springer-Verlag. DOI: 10.1007/978-3-642-00958-7_28 40

[23] Claudia Hauff, Djoerd Hiemstra, and Franciska de Jong. A survey of pre-retrieval query performance predictors. In *Proceeding of the 17th ACM conference on Information and knowledge management (CIKM 2008)*, pages 1419–1420, Napa Valley, California, USA, 2008. ACM. DOI: 10.1145/1458082.1458311 19, 22

[24] Claudia Hauff, Vanessa Murdock, and Ricardo Baeza-Yates. Improved query difficulty prediction for the web. In *Proceeding of the 17th ACM conference on Information and knowledge management (CIKM 2008)*, pages 439–448, Napa Valley, California, USA, 2008. ACM. DOI: 10.1145/1458082.1458142 29

[25] Ben He and Iadh Ounis. Inferring query performance using pre-retrieval predictors. In *Proceedings of the Symposium on String Processing and Information Retrieval*, pages 43–54. Springer Verlag, 2004. 17, 19, 20, 22, 23, 49

[26] Ben He and Iadh Ounis. Combining fields for query expansion and adaptive query expansion. *Information Processing and Management*, 43(5):1294–1307, 2007. DOI: 10.1016/j.ipm.2006.11.002 60

[27] Jiyin He, Martha Larson, and Maarten de Rijke. Using coherence-based measures to predict query difficulty. In *Proceedings of the European Conference on Information Retrieval (ECIR 2008)*, pages 689–694, 2008. DOI: 10.1007/978-3-540-78646-7_80 19, 21, 22

[28] Eric C. Jensen, Steven M. Beitzel, David Grossman, Ophir Frieder, and Abdur Chowdhury. Predicting query difficulty on the web by learning visual clues. In *Proceedings of the 28th annual international ACM SIGIR conference on Research and development in information retrieval (SIGIR 2005)*, pages 615–616, Salvador, Brazil, 2005. ACM. DOI: 10.1145/1076034.1076155 67

[29] Karen Sparck Jones, Stephen G. Walker, and Stephen E. Robertson. A probabilistic model of information retrieval: development and comparative experiments. *Information Processing and Management*, 36(6):779–808, 2000. DOI: 10.1016/S0306-4573(00)00015-7 9

[30] Josef Kittler, Mohamad Hatef, Robert P. W. Duin, and Jiri Matas. On combining classifiers. *IEEE Transactions on Pattern Analysis and Machine Intelligence*, 20:226–239, 1998. DOI: 10.1109/34.667881 39

[31] Giridhar Kumaran and James Allan. Selective user interaction. In *Proceedings of the 16th ACM conference on Conference on information and knowledge management (CIKM 2007)*, pages 923–926, Lisbon, Portugal, 2007. ACM. DOI: 10.1145/1321440.1321576 6, 55, 67

[32] Giridhar Kumaran and James Allan. Effective and efficient user interaction for long queries. In *Proceedings of the 31st annual international ACM SIGIR conference on Research and development in information retrieval (SIGIR 2008)*, pages 11–18, Singapore, Singapore, 2008. ACM. DOI: 10.1145/1390334.1390339 17

[33] Giridhar Kumaran and Vitor R. Carvalho. Reducing long queries using query quality predictors. In *Proceedings of the 32nd international ACM SIGIR conference on Research and development in information retrieval (SIGIR 2009)*, pages 564–571, Boston, MA, USA, 2009. ACM. DOI: 10.1145/1571941.1572038 63

[34] Kui-Lam Kwok. A new method of weighting query terms for ad-hoc retrieval. In *Proceedings of the 19th annual international ACM SIGIR conference on Research and development in information retrieval (SIGIR 1996)*, pages 187–195, Zurich, Switzerland, 1996. ACM. DOI: 10.1145/243199.243266 19

[35] John D. Lafferty and Chengxiang Zhai. Document language models, query models, and risk minimization for information retrieval. In *Proceedings of the 24th annual international ACM SIGIR conference on Research and development in information retrieval (SIGIR 2001)*, pages 111–119, New Orleans, Louisiana, United States, 2001. ACM. DOI: 10.1145/383952.383970 27, 41, 43

[36] Victor Lavrenko and W. Bruce Croft. Relevance based language models. In *Proceedings of the 24th annual international ACM SIGIR conference on Research and development in information retrieval (SIGIR 2001)*, pages 120–127, New Orleans, Louisiana, United States, 2001. ACM. DOI: 10.1145/383952.383972 43

[37] Yuanhua Lv and ChengXiang Zhai. Adaptive relevance feedback in information retrieval. In *Proceeding of the 18th ACM conference on Information and knowledge management (CIKM 2009)*, pages 255–264, Hong Kong, China, 2009. ACM. DOI: 10.1145/1645953.1645988 61, 67

[38] Donald Metzler and W. Bruce Croft. A Markov random field model for term dependencies. In *Proceedings of the 28th annual international ACM SIGIR conference on Research and development in information retrieval (SIGIR 2005)*, pages 472–479, Salvador, Brazil, 2005. ACM. DOI: 10.1145/1076034.1076115 22, 33

[39] Mandar Mitra, Amit Singhal, and Chris Buckley. Improving automatic query expansion. In *Proceedings of the 21st annual international ACM SIGIR conference on Research and development in information retrieval (SIGIR 1998)*, pages 206–214, Melbourne, Australia, 1998. ACM. DOI: 10.1145/290941.290995 33, 60

[40] Josiane Mothe and Ludovic Tanguy. Linguistic features to predict query difficulty. In *28th Annual International ACM SIGIR Conference on Research and Development in Information Retrieval (SIGIR 2005) Workshop on Query prediction and its applications*, Salvador - Bahia - Brazil, 2005. 17, 18, 66

[41] Paul Over. TREC-7 interactive track report. In *Proceedings of the 7th Text Retrieval Conference (TREC-7)*, pages 33–39. National Institute of Standards and Technology (NIST), 1998. 51

[42] Vassilis Plachouras, Ben He, and Iadh Ounis. University of glasgow at TREC 2004: Experiments in web, robust, and terabyte tracks with terrier. In *Proceedings of 10th Text REtrieval Conference (TREC-10)*, 2004. 20, 22

[43] Jay M. Ponte and W. Bruce Croft. A language modeling approach to information retrieval. In *Proceedings of the 21st annual international ACM SIGIR conference on Research and development in information retrieval (SIGIR 1998)*, pages 275–281, Melbourne, Australia, 1998. ACM. DOI: 10.1145/290941.291008 9

[44] Stephen Robertson. On GMAP and other transformations. In *Proceedings of the 15th ACM international conference on Information and knowledge management (CIKM 2006)*, pages 78–83, Arlington, Virginia, USA, 2006. ACM. DOI: 10.1145/1183614.1183630 5, 10

[45] Stephen E. Robertson. The probability ranking principle in IR. In *Readings in information retrieval*, pages 281–286. Morgan Kaufmann Publishers Inc., San Francisco, CA, USA, 1997. 41

[46] Joseph J. Rocchio. Relevance feedback in information retrieval. In *The SMART Retrieval System: Experiments in Automatic Document Processing*, pages 313 – 323, Englewood Cliffs, NJ, 1971. Prentice-Hall Inc. 60

[47] Gerard Salton and Christopher Buckley. Term-weighting approaches in automatic text retrieval. *Information Processing and Management*, pages 513–523, 1988. DOI: 10.1016/0306-4573(88)90021-0 9

[48] Anna Shtok, Oren Kurland, and David Carmel. Predicting query performance by query-drift estimation. In *Proceedings of the 2nd International Conference on Theory of Information Retrieval (ICTIR 2009)*, pages 305–312, Cambridge, UK, 2009. Springer-Verlag. DOI: 10.1007/978-3-642-04417-5_30 23, 33, 34, 35, 77

[49] Anna Shtok, Oren Kurland, and David Carmel. Using statistical decision theory and relevance models for query-performance prediction. In *Proceedings of the 33rd annual international ACM SIGIR conference on Research and development in information retrieval (SIGIR 2010)*, Geneva, Switzerland, 2010. ACM. 35, 36, 41, 42, 44, 45, 66, 77

[50] Fei Song and W. Bruce Croft. A general language model for information retrieval. In *Proceedings of the eighth international conference on Information and knowledge management (CIKM 1999)*, pages 316–321, Kansas City, Missouri, United States, 1999. ACM. DOI: 10.1145/319950.320022 27

[51] Scott Spangler and Jeffrey Kreulen. Knowledge base maintenance using knowledge gap analysis. In *Proceedings of the seventh ACM international conference on Knowledge discovery and data mining (KDD 2001)*, pages 462–466, San Francisco, California, 2001. ACM. DOI: 10.1145/502512.502582 58

[52] Jaime Teevan, Susan T. Dumais, and Daniel J. Liebling. To personalize or not to personalize: modeling queries with variation in user intent. In *Proceedings of the 31st annual international ACM SIGIR conference on Research and development in information retrieval (SIGIR 2008)*, pages 163–170, Singapore, Singapore, 2008. ACM. DOI: 10.1145/1390334.1390364 55, 67

[53] Stephen Tomlinson. Robust, Web and Terabyte Retrieval with Hummingbird Search Server at TREC 2004. In *Proceedings of TREC-13*, 2004. 32

[54] Cornelis J. van Rijsbergen. *Information Retrieval*. Butterworth-Heinemann, 1979. 31

[55] Vishwa Vinay. *The Relevance of Feedback for Text Retrieval*. PhD thesis, University College, London, March 2007. xi, 47, 48

[56] Vishwa Vinay, Ingemar J. Cox, Natasa Milic-Frayling, and Kenneth R. Wood. On ranking the effectiveness of searches. In *Proceedings of the 29th annual international ACM SIGIR conference on Research and development in information retrieval (SIGIR 2006)*, pages 398–404, Seattle, Washington, USA, 2006. ACM. DOI: 10.1145/1148170.1148239 23, 30, 31, 32, 49

[57] Ellen M. Voorhees. Overview of the TREC 2003 robust retrieval track. In *Proceedings of the Twelfth Text Retrieval Conference (TREC-12)*. National Institute of Standards and Technology (NIST), 2003. 4

[58] Ellen M. Voorhees. Overview of the TREC 2004 robust retrieval track. In *Proceedings of 13th Text Retrieval Conference (TREC-13)*. National Institute of Standards and Technology (NIST), 2004. 1, 4, 5

[59] Ellen M. Voorhees. Overview of the TREC 2005 robust retrieval track. In *Proceedings of the 14th Text Retrieval Conference (TREC-14)*. National Institute of Standards and Technology (NIST), 2005. DOI: 10.1145/1147197.1147205 4, 6

[60] Ellen M. Voorhees and Donna Harman. Overview of the sixth Text REtrieval conference (TREC-6). *Information Processing Management*, 36(1):3–35, 2000. DOI: 10.1016/S0306-4573(99)00043-6 5

[61] Ellen M. Voorhees and Donna K. Harman. Overview of the Tenth Text REtrieval Conference (TREC-10). In *Proceedings of the Tenth Text Retrieval Conference (TREC-10)*. National Institute of Standards and Technology (NIST), 2001. 9

[62] Ryen W. White, Matthew Richardson, Mikhail Bilenko, and Allison P. Heath. Enhancing web search by promoting multiple search engine use. In *Proceedings of the 31st annual international ACM SIGIR conference on Research and development in information retrieval (SIGIR 2008)*, pages 43–50, Singapore, Singapore, 2008. ACM. DOI: 10.1145/1390334.1390344 57

[63] Mattan Winaver, Oren Kurland, and Carmel Domshlak. Towards robust query expansion: model selection in the language modeling framework. In *Proceedings of the 30th annual international ACM SIGIR conference on Research and development in information retrieval (SIGIR 2007)*, pages 729–730, Amsterdam, The Netherlands, 2007. ACM. DOI: 10.1145/1277741.1277880 61

[64] Elad Yom-Tov, Shai Fine, David Carmel, and Adam Darlow. Learning to estimate query difficulty: including applications to missing content detection and distributed information retrieval. In *Proceedings of the 28th annual international ACM SIGIR conference on Research and development in information retrieval (SIGIR 2005)*, pages 512–519, Salvador, Brazil, 2005. ACM. DOI: 10.1145/1076034.1076121 23, 41, 58, 60, 67, 77

[65] Elad Yom-Tov, Shai Fine, David Carmel, and Adam Darlow. Metasearch and federation using query difficulty prediction. In *28th Annual International ACM SIGIR Conference on Research and Development in Information Retrieval (SIGIR 2005) Workshop on Query prediction and its applications*, Salvador, Brazil, 2005. 30, 31, 57, 67, 77

[66] Cheng Xiang Zhai, William W. Cohen, and John Lafferty. Beyond independent relevance: methods and evaluation metrics for subtopic retrieval. In *Proceedings of the 26th annual international ACM SIGIR conference on Research and development in information retrieval (SIGIR 2003)*, pages 10–17, Toronto, Canada, 2003. ACM. DOI: 10.1145/860435.860440 51

[67] Chengxiang Zhai and John Lafferty. A study of smoothing methods for language models applied to ad hoc information retrieval. In *Proceedings of the 24th annual international ACM SIGIR conference on Research and development in information retrieval (SIGIR 2001)*, pages 334–342, New Orleans, Louisiana, United States, 2001. ACM. DOI: 10.1145/383952.384019 22, 35

[68] Ying Zhao, Falk Scholer, and Yohannes Tsegay. Effective pre-retrieval query performance prediction using similarity and variability evidence. In *Proceedings of the European Conference on Information Retrieval (ECIR 2008)*, pages 52–64, 2008. DOI: 10.1007/978-3-540-78646-7_8 19, 21, 22, 23, 66

[69] Yun Zhou. *Retrieval Performance Prediction and Document Quality*. PhD thesis, University of Massachusetts, September 2007. xi, 23, 33, 35

[70] Yun Zhou and W. Bruce Croft. Ranking robustness: a novel framework to predict query performance. In *Proceedings of the 15th ACM international conference on Information and*

knowledge management (CIKM 2006), pages 567–574, Arlington, Virginia, USA, 2006. ACM. DOI: 10.1145/1183614.1183696 23, 30, 41

[71] Yun Zhou and W. Bruce Croft. Query performance prediction in web search environments. In *Proceedings of the 30th annual international ACM SIGIR conference on Research and development in information retrieval (SIGIR 2007)*, pages 543–550, Amsterdam, The Netherlands, 2007. ACM. DOI: 10.1145/1277741.1277835 29, 32, 35, 36, 41, 44, 61, 67

Authors' Biographies

DAVID CARMEL

David Carmel is a Research Staff Member at the Information Retrieval group at IBM Research Lab at Haifa. David earned his PhD in Computer Science from the Technion, Israel Institute of Technology in 1997. David's research is focused on search in the enterprise, query performance prediction, social search, and text mining. For several years David taught the Introduction to IR course at the CS department at Haifa university.

At IBM, David is a key contributor to IBM enterprise search offerings. David is a co-founder of the Juru search engine which provides integrated search capabilities to several IBM products, and was used as a search platform for several studies in TREC conferences. David has published more than 60 papers in Information retrieval and Web journals and conferences, and he serves in the Program Committee of many conferences (SIGIR, WWW, WSDM, CIKM, ECIR), journals (IR Journal), and workshops.

ELAD YOM-TOV

Elad Yom-Tov is a Research Staff Member at the Data Analytics department at IBM Research Lab at Haifa, Israel. The main focus of his work is research into methods for large-scale machine learning, with a recent focus on social analytics.

Prior to his current position he worked at Rafael Inc., where he applied machine learning to image processing. Elad is a graduate of Tel-Aviv University (B.Sc.) and the Technion, Haifa (M.Sc. and Ph.D). He is the author (with David Stork) of the Computer Manual to accompany Pattern Classification, a book and a Matlab toolbox on pattern classification. He has published over 40 papers on Machine Learning and its applications.

Elad's work in Information Retrieval includes query difficulty estimation, social tagging, and novelty detection.

BOTH

David and Elad published many papers on query performance prediction (64; 65; 12; 13; 48; 49), and organized a workshop on this subject in SIGIR 2005(11). Their paper on Learning to estimate query difficulty (64) won the Best Paper Award at SIGIR 2005.

Printed in the United States
by Baker & Taylor Publisher Services